Kaplan Publishing are constantly finding new ways to make a difference to yo exciting online resources really different to students looking fo

GW00546722

This book comes with free MyKaplan online resources so that you can study anytime, anywhere. This free online resource is not sold separately and is included in the price of the book.

Having purchased this book, you have access to the following online study materials:

CONTENT	ACCA (including FFA,FAB,FMA)		FIA (excluding FFA,FAB,FMA)	
	Text	Kit	Text	Kit
iPaper version of the book	✓	✓	✓	✓
Interactive electronic version of the book	✓			
Check Your Understanding Test with instant answers	✓			
Material updates	✓	✓	✓	✓
Latest official ACCA exam questions*		✓		
Extra question assistance using the signpost icon**		✓		
Timed questions with an online tutor debrief using clock icon*		✓		
Interim assessment including questions and answers	✓		✓	
Technical answers	✓	✓	✓	✓

* Excludes F1, F2, F3, F4, FAB, FMA and FFA; for all other papers includes a selection of questions, as released by ACCA

** For ACCA P1-P7 only

How to access your online resources

Kaplan Financial students will already have a MyKaplan account and these extra resources will be available to you online. You do not need to register again, as this process was completed when you enrolled. If you are having problems accessing online materials, please ask your course administrator.

If you are already a registered MyKaplan user go to www.MyKaplan.co.uk and log in. Select the 'add a book' feature and enter the ISBN number of this book and the unique pass key at the bottom of this card. Then click 'finished' or 'add another book'. You may add as many books as you have purchased from this screen.

If you purchased through Kaplan Flexible Learning or via the Kaplan Publishing website you will automatically receive an e-mail invitation to MyKaplan. Please register your details using this email to gain access to your content. If you do not receive the e-mail or book content, please contact Kaplan Flexible Learning.

If you are a new MyKaplan user register at www.MyKaplan.co.uk and click on the link contained in the email we sent you to activate your account. Then select the 'add a book' feature, enter the ISBN number of this book and the unique pass key at the bottom of this card. Then click 'finished' or 'add another book'.

Your Code and Information

This code can only be used once for the registration of one book online. This registration and your online content will expire when the final sittings for the examinations covered by this book have taken place. Please allow one hour from the time you submit your book details for us to process your request.

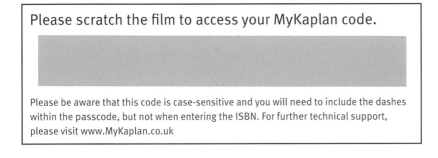

Please scratch the film to access your MyKaplan code.

Please be aware that this code is case-sensitive and you will need to include the dashes within the passcode, but not when entering the ISBN. For further technical support, please visit www.MyKaplan.co.uk

KAPLAN

PUBLISHING

INTERMEDIATE LEVEL

Paper MA2

Managing Costs and Finances

EXAM KIT

British Library Cataloguing-in-Publication Data

A catalogue record for this book is available from the British Library.

Published by
Kaplan Publishing UK
Unit 2 The Business Centre
Molly Millars Lane
Wokingham
Berkshire
RG41 2QZ

ISBN 978-1-78415-645-9

© Kaplan Financial Limited, 2016

Printed and bound in Great Britain

Acknowledgements

The past ACCA exam questions are the copyright of the Association of Chartered Certified Accountants. The original answers to the questions from June 2006 onwards were produced by the examiners themselves and have been adapted by Kaplan Publishing.

We are grateful to the Chartered Institute of Management Accountants and the Institute of Chartered Accountants in England and Wales for permission to reproduce past exam questions. The answers have been prepared by Kaplan Publishing.

INTRODUCTION

Packed with past exam questions, this book will help you to successfully prepare for your exam.

- Practice questions are grouped by syllabus topics

- All questions are of exam standard and format – this enables you to master the exam techniques.

CONTENTS

Quality and accuracy are of the utmost importance to us so if you spot an error in any of our products, please send an email to mykaplanreporting@kaplan.com with full details.

Our Quality Co-ordinator will work with our technical team to verify the error and take action to ensure it is corrected in future editions.

INDEX TO QUESTIONS AND ANSWERS

SYLLABUS AND REVISION GUIDANCE

Position of the paper in the overall syllabus

Knowledge of MA1, *Management Information*, at the introductory level is required before commencing study for MA2.

This paper provides the basic techniques required to enable candidates to develop knowledge and understanding of how to prepare, process and present basic cost information to support management in planning and decision making in a variety of business contexts.

Candidates will need a sound understanding of the methods and techniques introduced in this paper to ensure that they can take them further in subsequent papers. The methods introduced in this paper are revisited and extended in FMA, *Management Accounting.*

Syllabus

A **Management information** Section 1 and Section 6

   1   Management information requirements

   2   Cost accounting systems

   3   Cost classification

   4   Information for comparison

   5   Reporting management information

B **Cost recording** Section 2

   1   Accounting for materials

   2   Accounting for labour

   3   Accounting for other expenses

C **Costing techniques** Section 3

   1   Absorption costing

   2   Marginal costing

   3   Job and batch costing

   4   Process costing

   5   Service costing

D **Decision making** Section 4

   1   Cost- volume- profit analysis

   2   Factors affecting short term decision making

   3   Principles of discounted cash flow

E **Cash management** Section 5

   1   Nature of cash and cash flow

   2   Cash management

   3   Cash budgets

   4   Investing and financing

Planning your revision

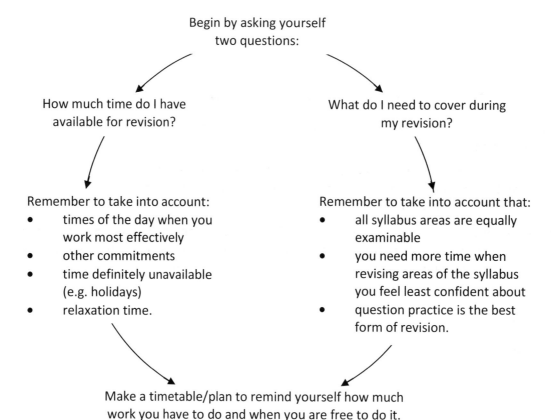

Revision techniques

- Go through your notes and textbook **highlighting the important points**.

- You might want to produce your own set of **summarised notes**.

- **List key words** for each topic to remind you of the essential concepts.

- **Practise exam-standard questions**, under timed conditions.

- **Rework questions** that you got completely wrong the first time, but only when you think you know the subject better.

- If you get stuck on topics, **find someone to explain** them to you (your tutor or a colleague, for example) .

- **Read recent articles** on the ACCA website or in the student magazine.

- **Read** good newspapers and professional journals.

THE EXAMINATION

Format of the examination

	Number of marks
50 objective test questions	100

Paper Based Exam

All questions will be in the form of multiple choice questions (this is where a candidate must choose one of four options, A through to D).

Computer Based Exam (CBE)

Each question is worth two marks each and can take one of four formats:

*   multiple choice questions (this is where a candidate must choose one of four options, A through to D)

*   multiple response questions (this is where the candidate must select more than one response from the options provided by clicking the appropriate tick boxes).

*   multiple response matching questions (this is where the candidate must match together related items. For example, statements on activity based costing might have to be categorised as either TRUE or FALSE)

*   number entry questions (this is where the candidate will be provided with an on-screen box into which he/she must enter the correct number)

For both exams

Questions assess all parts of the syllabus and will include both computational and non-computational elements.

*   Pass mark: 50%

*   Most recent pass rate: 67%

*   Total time allowed: 2 hours

Tips for sitting CBEs

The ACCA have provided the following advice for sitting a CBE:

*   The types of questions included in both paper-based exams and CBEs will be similar, but the way that each question is presented, and the way the answer is recorded, differs between the two methods. In a CBE, candidates record their answers on the same screen as the question is shown.

*   In a CBE you are presented with one question at a time, compared to the paper-based exam where you can see all questions at the same time. Displaying only one question at a time helps you focus on each question. Research tells us that the way we read information presented on a computer is different to how we read on paper. On the computer our eyes tend to jump around the screen rather than read it systematically as we would a printed page. Remember to take time to read the question carefully to ensure you don't miss any important information.

- Once you have entered your answer for a question, it is important to click on the 'Submit' button for your answer to be saved. You can revisit questions and change answers at any time until the exam duration has been reached – however, remember to click on 'Submit' to save your new answer once you have changed it.

- Do not spend a lot of time on questions you are unsure of; instead, move on and come back to these questions at the end of the exam.

- To make CBEs as user-friendly as possible we have incorporated features that will guide you through the exam. Part of the screen has been reserved for tools that will help you navigate between questions. In addition, questions that you have not attempted will be highlighted by an asterisk in the drop-down list of questions and you can quickly move to these questions by clicking on the relevant question number in the list. The exams also include a timer to show you how much time is remaining.

Preparing for the exam

- You can take a CBE **at any time during the year** – you do not need to wait for June and December exam sessions.

- Be sure you **understand how to use the software** before you start the exam. If in doubt, ask the assessment centre staff to explain it to you. **Questions are displayed on the screen** and **answers are entered using keyboard and mouse**.

- Don't panic if you realise you've answered a question incorrectly – **you can always go back and change your answer.**

- Read the questions carefully and work through any calculations required. If you don't know the answer, eliminate those options you know are incorrect and see if the answer becomes more obvious. Remember that only one answer to a multiple-choice question can be right!

- At the end of the examination, **you are given a certificate showing the result** you have achieved.

Tips for sitting a paper based exam

Many of the tips provided for CBEs will also be relevant to paper based exams such as:

- Don't panic if you realise you've answered a question incorrectly – **you can always go back and change your answer.**

- Read the questions carefully and work through any calculations required. If you don't know the answer, eliminate those options you know are incorrect and see if the answer becomes more obvious. Remember that only one answer to a multiple-choice question can be right!

There are some minor differences in the format of the exam such as:

- Questions will only take the form of multiple choice questions. So ensure that you have written a letter for every single question, even if some are only guesses. There is no negative marking in the exam.

- Answers are recorded on the candidate answer booklet. It will be important that you are not careless here and that you ensure that you are recording the correct answer next to the correct question

- Before you finish, you must **fill in the required information** on the front of your answer booklet. This will ask for information such as your candidate number and the script will not be marked unless this information is provided.

Section 1

MANAGEMENT INFORMATION

MANAGEMENT INFORMATION

1   Place a tick in the column to indicate which THREE of the following statements are correct?

	Correct?
Cost accounting can be used for inventory valuation to meet the requirements of internal reporting only	
Management accounting provides appropriate information for decision making, planning, control and performance evaluation	
Routine information can be used for both short-term and long-run decisions	
Financial accounting information can be used for internal reporting purposes	
Management accounting information must be presented in a prescribed industry format	

2   Which of the following is the correct definition of exception reporting?

   A   A report that is only produced when something out-of-the-ordinary has happened

   B   A report that highlights which divisions have had the best performance in the period

   C   A report that explains which controls managers are unhappy with

   D   A report that summarises the full year's performance for the business

3   For operational purposes, for a company operating a fleet of delivery vehicles, which of the following cost units would be most useful?

   A   Mile run

   B   Driver hour

   C   Tonne mile

   D   Kilogram carried

4   Which of the following would be included in the financial accounts, but may be excluded from the cost accounts?

   A   Direct material costs

   B   Depreciation of storeroom handling equipment

   C   Bank interest and charges

   D   Factory manager's salary

5 **An investment centre is best defined as:**

A   a centre within an enterprise with responsibilities for revenues, costs and capital investment, and whose performance is measured by its return on capital employed

B   a centre within an enterprise with responsibilities for revenues and costs, and whose performance is measured by its profitability

C   a centre within an enterprise where costs are collected before being analysed further

D   a centre within an enterprise whose performance is the responsibility of a specific manager

---

The following information relates to questions 6 to 9.

The following is a summary of entries in the work-in-progress (WIP) account in the cost ledger of XYZ.

Opening balance	$3,000 DR
Direct material used	$12,500
Direct labour charged to WIP	$21,500
Production overhead absorbed	$17,400
Transfers to finished goods	$49,000

---

6 **The balance of work-in-progress carried forward to the next period would be:**

A $6,100

B $5,750

C $600

D $5,400

7 **Place a tick in the correct columns to indicate the correct double entry for the materials charged to WIP:**

	WIP control	Finished goods control	Stores ledger control	Production overhead control
Debit				
Credit				

8 **Place a tick in the correct columns to indicate the correct double entry for the production overhead recovered in the period:**

	WIP control	Finished goods control	Stores ledger control	Production overhead control
Debit				
Credit				

9 The double entry for the transfer of finished goods would have been:

	WIP control	Finished goods control	Cost of sales account	Production overhead control
Debit				
Credit				

10 Which one of the following may be included in the cost accounts but excluded from the financial accounts?

A   Depreciation of equipment

B   Distribution expenses

C   Factory manager's salary

D   Notional rent

11 In an interlocking system, what would be the entry for the issue of indirect material from inventory?

	Account debited	Account credited
A	Material inventory	Production overhead
B	Material inventory	Work-in-progress
C	Production overhead	Material inventory
D	Work-in-progress	Material inventory

12 What is the correct entry in the cost ledger to record the over-absorption of production overhead?

	Debit	Credit
A	Over-absorbed production overhead a/c	Production overhead a/c
B	Over-absorbed production overhead a/c	Work-in-progress a/c
C	Production overhead a/c	Over-absorbed production overhead a/c
D	Work-in-progress a/c	Over-absorbed production overhead a/c

13 Consider the following incomplete statements relating to management information:

(i)   clear to the user

(ii)   detailed and completely accurate

(iii)   provided whatever the cost

(iv)   relevant for purpose

Which of the above are necessary features of useful management information?

A   (i) and (ii)

B   (i) and (iv)

C   (ii) and (iv)

D   (i), (ii) and (iii)

14 Place a tick in the column to indicate which TWO of the following are features of graphical user interfaces:

	Features of graphical users interfaces
Icons	
Keyboard	
Optical mark reading	
Pull-down menu	

15 Which one of the following is a common feature of cost accounting but not financial accounting?

    A   Control accounts

    B   Cost classification

    C   Marginal costing

    D   Periodic stocktaking

16 Cost centres are:

    A   units of product or service for which costs are ascertained

    B   amounts of expenditure attributable to various activities

    C   functions or locations for which costs are ascertained and related to cost units

    D   a section of an organisation for which budgets are prepared and control exercised

17 What is the purpose of management information?

    A   Planning only

    B   Planning and control only

    C   Planning, control and decision making only

    D   Planning, control, decision making and research and development

18 Which of the following is a feature of an interlocking bookkeeping system?

    A   One set of ledger accounts

    B   No control accounts

    C   Cost ledger contains asset and liability accounts

    D   Separate cost and financial ledgers

19 Place a tick in the column to indicate which THREE of the following are used for the capture and storage of management accounting data by computer:

	Used to capture and store data
Bar code	
Disk	
Printer	
Tape	

20 In an integrated cost and financial accounting system, what would be the entry to record direct labour costs being charged to production?

	Debit	Credit
A	Financial ledger control	Work-in-progress
B	Production overhead	Wages control
C	Finished goods	Work-in-progress
D	Work-in-progress	Wages control

21 The management accountant of X has written a report assessing the cost savings that could be made if the company were to invest in new technology.

In which area will the report primarily aid the management of X?

A Budgeting

B Control

C Decision making

D Monitoring

22 Which of the following only contains essential features of useful management information?

A Accurate, clear, presented in report format

B Timely, reliable, supported by calculations

C Regular, complete, communicated in writing

D Clear, accurate, relevant for its purpose

23 What is an interlocking bookkeeping system?

A A single, combined system containing both cost accounting and financial accounting records.

B A system combining cost accounting and management accounting.

C A system supported by prime entry records.

D A system where separate accounts are kept for cost accounting and for financial accounting.

24 Which of the following best describes a profit centre?

A Part of a business where management makes investment decisions.

B Part of a business that provides a service to other parts of the business.

C Part of a business where finished products are manufactured.

D Part of a business where management is responsible for revenues and costs.

25 **In a large company, which of the following activities may be the responsibility of an accounting technician?**

A   Calculating cost variances

B   Making capital investment decisions

C   Approving budgets

D   Allocating warehouse space

26 **Which of the following are characteristics of management accounting information?**

(i)   Non-financial as well as financial

(ii)   Used by all stakeholders

(iii)   Concerned with cost control only

(iv)   Not legally required

A   (i) and (iv)

B   (ii) and (iii)

C   (i), (ii) and (iii)

D   (ii), (iii) and (iv)

27 **Are the following statements true?**

(1)   Completed questionnaires, as part of a market research survey, are examples of data

(2)   Monthly management accounting reports, resulting from the processing of financial transactions, are examples of information

A   Both statements are not true

B   Only statement (1) is true

C   Only statement (2) is true

D   Both statements are true

28 **Place a tick in the column to indicate which TWO of the following statements are true:**

	True
In an integrated accounting system there will be a cost ledger control account	
An integrated accounting system has one combined set of ledger accounts	
An interlocking accounting system has separate cost and financial ledger accounts	

COST CLASSIFICATION AND COST BEHAVIOUR

29   **Prime cost comprises:**

A   all variable costs

B   direct labour and material only

C   direct labour, direct material and direct expense

D   direct labour, direct material and production overhead

30   **A semi-variable cost is one that:**

A   increases in direct proportion to output

B   remains constant irrespective of the level of output

C   contains an element of both fixed and variable cost

D   increases throughout the year

31   **Which of the costs listed below is NOT a fixed cost?**

A   Insurance

B   Business rates

C   Depreciation – based on straight-line method

D   Materials used in production

32   **Production overhead comprises:**

A   variable overheads only

B   indirect labour, indirect material and indirect expenses related to production activity

C   indirect expenses only

D   indirect labour and material related to the production activity

33   **Use a tick to indicate which of the following provides the correct definition of a direct cost is:**

	Correct definition
A cost which cannot be influenced by its budget holder	
Expenditure which can be economically identified with a specific cost unit	
Cost which needs to be apportioned to a cost centre	
The highest proportion of the total cost of a product	

34   **Which of the following items would be treated as an indirect cost?**

A   Wood used to make a chair

B   Metal used for the legs of a chair

C   Fabric to cover the seat of the chair

D   Staples to fix the fabric to the seat of the chair

35   The following graph represents which type of cost?

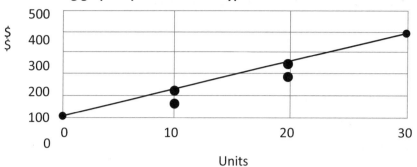

A   Fixed cost

B   Variable cost

C   Semi-variable cost

D   Stepped cost

36   The following data relate to the overhead expenditure of contract cleaners at two activity levels:

Square metres cleaned	12,750	15,100
Overheads	$73,950	$83,585

Using the high-low method, the estimate of the overhead cost if 16,200 square metres are to be cleaned is $_____

37   The following data relate to two output levels of a department:

Machine hours	17,000	18,500
Overheads	$246,500	$251,750

The amount of fixed overheads is:

A $5,250

B $59,500

C $187,000

D $246,500

38   The following summary data is provided for two periods:

	Production costs	Output
Period 1	$48,981	29,720 units
Period 2	$55,893	35,480 units

Using the high-low method, what are the estimated fixed costs per period?

A $6,912

B $13,317

C $24,214

D $26,326

39 A particular cost is fixed in total for a period.

What is the effect on the cost per unit of a reduction in activity of 50%?

A   Cost per unit increases by 50%

B   Cost per unit reduces by 50%

C   Cost per unit increases by 100%

D   Cost per unit is unchanged

40 **Which description best fits the cost curve?**

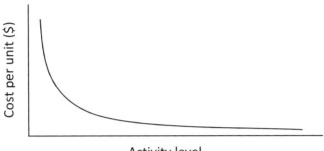

A   Direct material cost per unit

B   Fixed production cost per unit

C   Direct labour cost per unit

D   Variable production cost per unit

41 **What are conversion costs?**

A   Direct costs only

B   Indirect costs only

C   Production costs excluding direct materials

D   Rework costs

42 Total production costs and output over three periods have been:

Period	Production costs	Output
1	$230,485	12,610 units
2	$254,554	14,870 units
3	$248,755	14,350 units

The estimated variable production costs per unit if the high-low method is $_____ (round to two decimal places)

43 A particular cost is classified as being 'semi-variable'.

If activity increases by 10% what will happen to the cost per unit?

A   Increases

B   Reduces but not in proportion to the change in activity

C   Reduces in proportion to the change in activity

D   Remains constant

The following information relates to questions 44 to 46.

Marlows manufactures one product – jeans. As management accountant at Marlows you have determined the following information:

		$/unit
Direct materials		10
Direct labour		29
Direct expenses		3
Factory overheads	– variable	7
	– fixed	5
Non-manufacturing overheads	– variable	2
	– fixed	4
		60

Profit is one third of total cost.

44   What is the final selling price?

   A $56

   B $72

   C $80

   D $90

45   What is the variable cost?

   A $48 per unit

   B $42 per unit

   C $51 per unit

   D $49 per unit

46   What is the prime cost?

   A $54 per unit

   B $60 per unit

   C $42 per unit

   D $49 per unit

47 Costs have been recorded at three output levels:

Production output	100,000 units	105,000 units	110,000 units
Total costs	$207,000	$213,000	$218,200

Using the high–low method, what is the variable cost per unit (to two decimal places of $)?

A $0.89

B $1.04

C $1.12

D $1.20

48 **Which of the descriptions best suits the graph?**

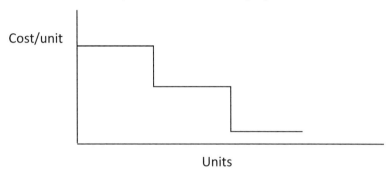

Cost/unit falls due to:

A a learning curve effect

B overtime being worked

C the availability of discounts for materials

D actual overheads being more than expected

49 A company carries out production in accordance with the special requirements of each customer.

Which costing method is MOST appropriate?

A Batch costing

B Job costing

C Process costing

D Service costing

50 Total costs incurred by a business may be expressed as:

$y = a + bx$

where

y represents the total costs

a represents the total fixed costs

b represents the variable costs per unit

x represents the number of units of output

A company has variable costs of $12.20 per unit and total costs, for output of 7,400 units in a period, of $156,980.

Using the above formula and information, what are the total fixed costs in the period?

A $156,980

B $66,700

C $90,280

D $247,260

51 A company currently produces 6,000 units of its single product each period, incurring total variable costs of $60,000 and fixed costs of $42,000. Production will increase to 8,000 units per period if the company expands capacity, resulting in changes both to the variable costs per unit and to the total fixed costs. For production of 8,000 units per period total variable costs would be $76,000 and fixed costs $50,000.

What is the reduction in total cost per unit comparing the costs for 8,000 units per period with the unit costs currently being incurred?

A $0.50

B $0.75

C $1.25

D $2.08

52 The following is an extract from the list of accounts of a washing machine manufacturer:

	Cost codes
Direct materials	1000 – 1999
Direct labour	2000 – 2999
Direct expenses	3000 – 3999
Production overheads	4000 – 4999

Which of the following are coded correctly?

	Code	Description
A	4160	wages of operatives who work on the product
B	2430	wages of production department supervisor
C	1670	cleaning materials
D	3020	royalties for component used in manufactured product

53 Machine parts are assembled in a factory. One of the components used in assembling machine part MP7 is component C6.

Which of the following is an example of a cost unit in the factory?

A   A unit of component C6

B   A unit of machine part MP7

C   The cost per unit of component C6

D   The cost per unit of machine part MP7

54 **Place a tick in the column to indicate which TWO of the following cost classifications can be applied to the straight-line depreciation of office equipment:**

	Apply to straight line depreciation
Indirect	
Period	
Production	
Variable	

55 The costs incurred in the manufacture of 1,000 units of a product are:

Direct materials $4,000

Direct labour $6,000

Variable overheads $2,000

Fixed overheads $8,000

If output increases by 25%, what will be the effect, if any, on the total cost per unit?

A   Decrease by $1.60 per unit

B   Decrease by $2.00 per unit

C   Decrease by $5.00 per unit

D   No effect

56 **Place a tick in the column to indicate which TWO of the following are expenses that may be part of the cost accounts, but not of the financial accounts:**

	Only appear in cost accounts
Cash discounts available to customers	
Interest charged to products based on average inventory	
Notional rent for the use, by different cost centres, of company-owned buildings	
Trade discounts received from suppliers	

57 A particular cost has been classified as 'semi-variable'.

How will the average cost per unit of activity be affected by a 20% reduction in the level of activity?

A   Decrease by less than 20%

B   Decrease by more than 20%

C   Increase by less than 25%

D   Increase by more than 25%

58 **A business designs, stitches and assembles tailored business suits and sells these directly to the public over the internet. It uses a mixture of cost units and cost centres. Which of the following would be deemed to be a cost centre (choose all that apply)?**

	Cost units
Cost per length of cloth	
Cost of the design department	
Cost of the stitching team	
Cost per dress	
Cost of delivery	

Section 2

COST RECORDING

ACCOUNTING FOR MATERIALS

The following information relates to questions 59 to 60.

The inventory record for component BXY for the month of January showed:

	Receipts	Value $	Issues
Opening inventory	500	1,250	
4 January	1,000	2,750	
11 January	1,600	4,480	
18 January	1,200	3,480	
19 January			2,100
25 January	1,500	4,350	
31 January			1,800

59 Using the FIFO method of pricing issues, the cost of issues during the month was:

   A $11,250

   B $10,800

   C $10,850

   D $11,300

60 Using the LIFO method of pricing issues, the value of inventory at 31 January?

   A $4,100

   B $3,720

   C $5,120

   D $3,950

61 Using the cumulative weighted average cost method of pricing, at what price would the issues on 31 January be made?

   (Calculate to two decimal places.)

   A $3.00

   B $2.95

   C $2.90

   D $2.83

62 A company business requires 600 units of material for its output. However, 5% of all materials used in production are lost in the production process.

To the nearest whole unit, the number of units of materials that must be put into the process is _____ units.

The following information relates to questions 63 and 64.

Turner has the following inventory record:

Date		Units	Cost
1 March	Opening inventory	100 units	at $3.00/unit
3 March	Receipt	200 units	at $3.50/unit
8 March	Issue	250 units	
15 March	Receipt	300 units	at $3.20/unit
17 March	Receipt	200 units	at $3.30/unit
21 March	Issue	500 units	
23 March	Receipt	450 units	at $3.10/unit
27 March	Issue	350 units	

63 The valuation of closing inventory if LIFO is used is $_____

64 The valuation of issues using cumulative the weighted average method of inventory valuation at each issue is $_____

65 A business expects wastage to be 3% of material input. During January, actual material input was 12,000 kg of materials and 11,520 kg of finished output was produced.

What is the difference between the actual and expected wastage rate for materials?

A   1%

B   2%

C   3%

D   4%

66 Insert a tick to indicate which TWO of the following costs would NOT be considered to be sound procedures implemented in order to reduce materials wastage and discrepancies:

	Poor procedures
Ordering in bulk in order to reduce order costs	
Having one staff member responsible for ordering and checking deliveries	
Demanding material requisition notes from production departments	
Performing regular inventory volume checks	
Using goods received notes to update inventory records	

67   A company uses the first-in, first-out (FIFO) method to price issues of raw material to production and to value its closing inventory.

   Which of the following statements best describes the first-in, first-out method?

   A   The last materials received will be the first issued to production.

   B   The first materials issued will be priced at the cost of the most recently received materials.

   C   The last materials issued will be those that were most recently received.

   D   The first materials issued will be priced at the cost of the earliest goods still in inventory.

68   **If a company is using the first-in, first-out method for material issues at a time when material prices are rising this will mean which of the following?**

   A   Production costs will be lower and profits will be higher than if the last-in, first-out method had been used.

   B   Production costs will be higher and profits will be lower than if the last-in, first-out method had been used.

   C   Production costs will be lower and profits will be lower than if the last-in, first-out method had been used.

   D   Production costs will be higher and profits will be higher than if the last-in, first-out method had been used.

69   A company produces one product, the X100, with following inventory information:

Usage per month	2,000 maximum
	1,800 minimum
Delivery period	2 months maximum
	1 month minimum
Re-order quantity	3,000 units

   The re-order level would be calculated as:

   A   4,200

   B   4,000

   C   3,700

   D   4,400

70   **When charging direct material cost to a job or process, the details would be taken from which document?**

   A   Purchase requisition

   B   Material requisition

   C   Goods received note

   D   Purchase order

71 A company uses the economic order quantity formula (EOQ) to establish its optimal re-order quantity for its single raw material. The following data relates to the inventory costs:

Purchase price: $15 per item

Carriage costs: $50 per order (irrespective of order size)

Ordering costs: $5 per order

Storage costs: 10% of purchase price plus $0.20 per unit per annum

Annual demand is 4,000 units.

What is the EOQ to the nearest whole unit?

A   153 units

B   170 units

C   485 units

D   509 units

72 In the formula $Q = \sqrt{2C_oD/C_h}$, if Co = $20, D = 24,000 and Q = 400, then Ch is $_____

73 A company uses two very similar types of fixing bracket, Z99 and Z100. When the company undertakes an inventory check it finds some differences as shown below:

Product	Inventory record	Inventory count
Z99	100	79
Z100	80	101

What is the most likely reason for the differences between the inventory record and the inventory count for each bracket?

A   Production was higher than expected

B   Some brackets were damaged during production

C   A customer asked the company to supply some extra brackets of both types

D   Some brackets were put in the incorrect storage racks

74 Hill Company wishes to minimise its inventory costs. At the moment its re-order quantity is 1,000 units. Order costs are $10 per order and holding costs are $0.10 per unit per month. Hill Company estimates annual demand to be 15,000 units.

What is the optimal re-order quantity (to the nearest 100 units)?

A   500 units

B   1,000 units

C   1,200 units

D   1,700 units

75   Insert a tick to indicate which FOUR of the following costs would be needed in order to
      calculate the economic order quantity

	Used in calculating the EOQ
The cost of storing materials	
The cost of interest incurred in financing materials	
The purchase of inventory	
The cost of ordering materials	
The cost of insuring materials	

76   **If a company wanted to ensure that its cost of production included the most recent cost
      for material, it would use:**

      A   periodic weighted average cost

      B   first-in, first-out (FIFO)

      C   cumulative weighted average cost

      D   last-in, first-out (LIFO)

77   **Failure to record inventory returned to stores will result in which of the following if a
      physical stocktake were not undertaken?**

	Inventory quantity	*Production costs*
A	Higher than shown on record card	Higher than it should be
B	Lower than shown on record card	Higher than it should be
C	Lower than shown on record card	Lower than it should be
D	Higher than shown on record card	Lower than it should be

78   **The following are statements relating to raw material pricing in a situation where raw
      material prices are rising consistently. Select whether the statements are true or false:**

	True	False
Production costs will be lower using weighted average pricing rather than LIFO.		
Profit will be higher using LIFO pricing rather than FIFO.		
Inventory values will be lower using FIFO pricing rather than weighted average.		

79   A company orders a particular raw material in order quantities of 250 units. No safety
      inventory is held, the cost of holding inventory is $3 per unit per annum and the annual
      demand is 2,500 units.

      What is the total annual stockholding cost of the material?

      A $375

      B $750

      C $3,750

      D $7,500

80 **Which of the following is NOT relevant to the calculation of the economic order quantity of a raw material?**

A   Ordering cost

B   Purchase price

C   Stockholding cost

D   Usage

81 A company has the following information about its inventory:

Usage per month	3,000 maximum
	2,700 minimum
Delivery period	2 months maximum
	1 month minimum
Re-order quantity	4,500 units
Re-order level	6,000 units

The maximum inventory control level would be calculated as _____ units

82 The order quantity of a raw material is 2,000 kg. Safety inventory of 1,200 kg is held. The cost of holding the raw material is $1.20 per kg per annum.

What is the total annual stockholding cost of the raw material?

A $1,200

B $1,920

C $2,640

D $3,840

83 **Indicate using a tick which TWO of the following documents are matched with the goods received note in the buying process:**

	Matched with the good received note
Invoice from supplier	
Purchase order	
Purchase requisition	
Stores requisition	

84 The following transactions relate to a raw material for a period:

Day	Transaction	Units	Total value ($)
1	Balance b/f	100	500
3	Issue	40	
4	Receipt	50	275
6	Receipt	50	300
7	Issue	70	

The *periodic* weighted average method is used to price material issues.

The value of the issue on Day 7 is $_____ (round to two decimal places)

The following information relates to questions 85 and 86.

The re-order level of Material M is 1,600 kg and the order quantity is 1,400 kg. Lead times and usage are as follows:

Lead time:	minimum	1 week
	average	1.5 weeks
	maximum	2 weeks
Usage:	minimum	600 kg per week
	average	700 kg per week
	maximum	800 kg per week

85 **What is the maximum inventory control level of Material M?**

A 1,400 kg

B 1,950 kg

C 2,400 kg

D 3,000 kg

86 **What is the minimum inventory control level of Material M?**

A Nil

B 350 kg

C 550 kg

D 1,000 kg

87 **Which of the following statements is correct?**

A A stores ledger account will be updated from a goods received note only.

B A stores requisition will only detail the type of product required by a customer.

C The term 'lead time' is best used to describe the time between receiving an order and paying for it.

D To make an issue from stores authorisation should be required.

88 The following relate to the management of raw materials:

(i) holding costs per unit of inventory would increase

(ii) the economic order quantity would decrease

(iii) average inventory levels would increase

(iv) total ordering costs would decrease

Which of the above would result from the introduction of buffer (safety) inventory?

A (iii) only

B (ii) and (iii) only

C (ii), (iii) and (iv) only

D (i), (ii), (iii) and (iv)

89 What is the purpose of calculating an economic order quantity (EOQ) for a raw material?

A   To minimise the stockholding quantity of the material

B   To minimise the stockholding costs of the material

C   To minimise the total cost of purchasing and storing the material

D   To enable the re-order level of the material to be established

90 Select whether the following statements describing the effect of raw material pricing policy in a situation where prices are rising consistently are true or false

	True	False
Inventory values will be higher using last-in first-out (LIFO) rather than weighted average.		
Profit will be lower using weighted average rather than first-in first-out (FIFO).		

91 Insert a tick to indicate which ONE of the following documents may be used to record raw materials sent back to stores from production when accounting for raw materials:

	Raw materials returns
Goods received note	
Materials returned note	
Materials requisition note	
Delivery note	

92 Material M is used by a manufacturer. Inventory of Material M at 1 May was valued at a cost of $3,302 (260 kg at $12.70 per kg). 500 kg were purchased on 7 May for $6,500. 410 kg of Material M were used in production during the month. The LIFO method is applied at the end of each month.

In the following table, indicate what amount would be charged to each account in the cost accounting system for the issues of Material M during the month and also indicate whether it would be a debit or a credit:

	$5,252	$5,330	Debit	Credit
Material inventory				
Work-in-progress				

93 How is the re-order level calculated if stock-outs are to be avoided?

A   Maximum usage × Maximum lead time

B   Maximum usage × Minimum lead time

C   Minimum usage × Maximum lead time

D   Minimum usage × Minimum lead time

94   The following information relates to a raw material inventory item:

Economic order quantity   800 units (established using the formula $\sqrt{\dfrac{2cd}{h}}$)

Demand   12,000 units per annum

Cost of holding inventory $1.50 per unit per annum

What is the cost of placing an order?

A $27

B $40

C $71

D $80

95   At the beginning of a period, 150 units of a component, which had been purchased at $6.40 per unit, were in inventory. During the period, 290 units of the component were purchased (160 units at $6.50 followed by 130 units at $6.90). 315 units of the component were issued to production at the end of the period when the cost of the 125 units remaining was $800.

Which method is being used to price the issues of the component?

A   First-in First-out

B   Last-in First-out

C   Periodic weighted average

D   Weighted average

96   A wholesaler uses the first-in first-out (FIFO) method of pricing inventory issues at each month end. The following details, relating to Product Z, are provided for a month:

Opening balance   860 units at a total cost of $1,892
Purchases   1,000 units at a total cost of $2,250
Sales   910 units

What is the cost of sales of Product Z in the month?

A $2,002.00

B $2,004.50

C $2,045.00

D $2,047.50

97   **Indicate which of the following are relevant in the calculation of the maximum inventory control level?**

	Used in calculating the maximum inventory control level
Maximum lead time	
Minimum usage	
Reorder level	
Reorder quantity	

ACCOUNTING FOR LABOUR

98   Gross wages incurred in a cost centre for the month of January showed:

		$
Ordinary time	direct employees	27,500
	indirect employees	6,500
Overtime	direct employees	
	basic	4,500
	premium	2,250
Special conditions allowance	direct employees	1,300
	indirect employees	450
Shift allowance	direct employees	2,000
Sick pay	direct employees	750

The overtime is a regular feature.

The direct wages for January would be $_____

99   RCW operates a bonus scheme based on time saved against a predetermined time allowance for actual output. In Week 6, an operative produced 750 units of 'R' in 32 hours. The standard allowance is 20 units of 'R' per hour.

The time saved by this employee in Week 6 on 'R' production was:

A   6.50

B   4.75

C   5.50

D   5.90

100   H&H operates an incentive scheme based on differential piecework. Employees are paid on the following basis

Weekly output up to:	600 units	–	$0.40 per unit
	601 – 650 units	–	$0.50 per unit
	650 units +	–	$0.75 per unit

with only the additional units qualifying for the higher rates. This is paid only upon production meeting quality standards. In Week 17, an employee produced 660 good units.

The gross pay for the week would be:

A $260.40

B $272.50

C $325.75

D $488.25

101   **H&H employed on average 55 employees during the year. There had been 8 leavers all of whom were replaced. The company's labour turnover ratio was _____ %** (round to two decimal places)

102 Which of the following relates to the cost of replacing labour due to high employee turnover?

    A   Improving working conditions

    B   Suffering the learning curve effect

    C   Provision of a pension

    D   Provision of welfare services

103 Which of the following methods of remuneration is not an incentive-based scheme?

    A   Straight piecework

    B   High day rate

    C   Group bonus

    D   Differential piecework

104 The following information relates to a small production unit during a period:

Budgeted hours	9,500 hours
Actual hours worked	9,200 hours
Standard hours of work produced	9,300 hours

What is the efficiency ratio for the period to the nearest 1%?

    A   97%

    B   98%

    C   99%

    D   101%

105 A job is budgeted to require 3,300 productive hours after incurring 25% idle time. If the total labour cost budgeted for the job is $36,300, the labour cost per hour is $_____ (round to two decimal places)

106 Which of the following would be classified as direct labour?

    A   Personnel manager in a company servicing cars

    B   Bricklayer in a construction company

    C   General manager in a DIY shop

    D   Maintenance manager in a company producing cameras

107 Which of the following statements is correct?

    A   Idle time cannot be controlled because it is always due to external factors

    B   Idle time is always controllable because it is due to internal factors

    C   Idle time is always due to inefficient production staff

    D   Idle time is not always the fault of production staff

108 Employee A is a carpenter and normally works 36 hours per week. The standard rate of pay is $6.60 per hour. A premium of 50% of the basic hourly rate is paid for all overtime hours worked. During the last week of October, Employee A worked for 42 hours. The overtime hours worked were for the following reasons:

Machine breakdown   4 hours

To complete a special job at the request of the customer: 2 hours

How much of Employee A's earnings for the last week of October would have been treated as direct wages?

A $237.60

B $257.40

C $277.20

D $283.80

109 A company makes a product for which the standard hour is 0.5. The budgeted production hours for a given week were 820. During the week the production staff were able to produce 380 units of product. Staff worked and were paid for 800 hours. During the week 20 production hours were lost due to a shortage of material.

The efficiency ratio was therefore:

A   95.00%

B   95.12%

C   97.44%

D   97.50%

110 A company has calculated that its activity ratio is 103.5% and that its efficiency ratio is 90%.

Therefore its capacity ratio will be:

A   86.96%

B   93.15%

C   115.00%

D   193.50%

111 A company pays direct operatives a basic wage of $8.50 per hour plus a productivity bonus. The bonus is calculated as:

[(Time allowed – Time taken) × (Basic rate per hour ÷ 3)]

The time allowed is 2.4 minutes per unit of output. An operative produced 1,065 units in a $37^1/_2$ hour week.

What were the total earnings of the operative in the week?

A $318.75

B $333.20

C $340.40

D $362.10

112 A company operates a piecework scheme to pay its staff. The staff receive $0.20 for each unit produced. However the company guarantees that every member of staff receive at least $15 per day.

Shown below is the number of units produced by Operator A during a recent week:

Day	Monday	Tuesday	Wednesday	Thursday	Friday
Units produced	90	70	75	60	90

What are Operator A's earnings for the week?

A $75.00

B $77.00

C $81.00

D $152.00

113 Which of the following would be classified as an overhead?

A Overtime premium when the overtime was worked at the customer's request

B Overtime premium when the overtime worked was because of a machine breakdown

C Payments to staff on a piecework scheme

D The basic pay relating to overtime hours

114 A company employs 20 direct production operatives and 10 indirect staff in its manufacturing department. The normal operating hours for all employees is 38 hours per week and all staff are paid $5 per hour. Overtime hours are paid at the basic rate plus 50%.

During a particular week all employees worked for 44 hours.

The amount charged to production overhead would be $_____

115 A differential piecework scheme has a basic rate of $0.50 per unit. Output in addition to 500 units is paid at higher rates. The premiums over and above the basic rate, which apply only to additional units over the previous threshold, are:

Output (units)	Premium (per unit)
501 – 600	$0.05
above 600	$0.10

The total amount paid if output is 620 units is $_____

116 Insert a tick to indicate which TWO of the following is usually included in direct labour costs:

	Direct labour cost
Overtime hours of direct operatives at basic rate	
Overtime premiums of factory employees	
Productive time of direct operatives	
Training of direct operatives	

117 Insert a tick to indicate which TWO of the following labour records may be used to allocate costs to the various cost units in a factory:

	Used to allocate costs
Employee record card	
Attendance record card	
Timesheet	
Job card	

118 How is the activity (production volume) ratio calculated?

A Actual hours ÷ Budgeted hours

B Budgeted hours ÷ Actual hours

C Standard hours for actual output ÷ Actual hours

D Standard hours for actual output ÷ Budgeted hours

119 Which of the following may be used to support claims for overtime payments for salaried staff?

A Employee record cards

B Job cards

C Payslips

D Timesheets

120 The gross wages of the direct operatives in a production cost centre for a period are analysed as follows:

	Direct operatives ($)
Productive hours at basic rate	37,640
Overtime premium	2,440
Idle time	590
Group bonuses	3,130

How much of the gross wages would normally be accounted for as direct labour?

A $37,640

B $40,080

C $40,670

D $43,210

121 The direct labour capacity ratio for a period was 104%.

What could have caused this?

A Actual hours worked being greater than budgeted hours

B Actual hours worked being less than budgeted hours

C Standard time for actual output being greater than budgeted hours

D Standard time for actual output being less than budgeted hours

122 An incentive scheme is in operation for each direct worker in a factory. The basic rate of pay is $8 per hour for an 8-hour day with a bonus if hours worked are less than the standard hours for the output achieved. The bonus is 50% of the time saved against standard, paid at the basic rate. A single product is manufactured and the standard time is 10 minutes per unit.

What is the bonus for a worker who manufactures 60 units in an 8-hour day?

A $0

B $4

C $8

D $16

123 The following data relates to production activity in a cost centre for a period:

	Budget	Actual
Output (units)	9,600	9,400
Labour (hours)	2,400	2,320

What was the efficiency ratio in the period (to one decimal place)?

A   96.7%

B   97.9%

C   98.7%

D   101.3%

124 **Insert a tick to indicate which TWO of the following are accounts used in the financial accounting systems to record wages and salaries costs:**

	Used in the financial accounting system
Wages and salaries control account	
Wages and salaries payable account	
Wages and salaries overtime account	
Wages and salaries overhead account	

125 An employee who works directly on production works a standard 40 hour week. They are paid $10.50 per hour and overtime is paid at time and a half. During a week the employee worked 50 hours and on top of the basic pay and overtime received a bonus of $100.

What is the direct cost of labour for this employee?

A $677.50

B $525.50

C $520.00

D $577.50

ACCOUNTING FOR OTHER EXPENSES

126 DF operates from three main sites. In analysing its costs (overheads) it uses a nine-digit coding system. A sample from the coding manual shows:

Site		Expenditure type		Function	
Whitby	100	Rent	410	Purchasing	600
Scarborough	200	Power	420	Finance	610
York	300	Heat and light	430	Production	620
		Travel costs	500	Sales	630
		Telephone and postage	520		

The order of coding is: site/expense/function

An invoice for the Whitby site for power would be coded as ____ /____ /____

127 **HockeySkill manufactures hockey sticks. Insert a tick to indicate which FIVE of the following costs would be classified as part of the production overhead:**

	Production overhead costs
Wood used as raw material	
Rubber covers for handles	
Depreciation	
Power	
Sales manager's salary	
Labour in assembly department	
Oils and greases	
Telephone and postage	
Insurance of plant	
Supervisory labour	

128 HockeySkill purchased a new machine in January 20X3. The cost of the machine was $45,000. The company policy is to depreciate machinery on a machine hour basis. The machine has an estimated life of five years. The machine is estimated to operate for 3,000 hours per annum. In the period ended four months to April 30, it operated for 810 machine hours.

The depreciation charge for the period would be:

A $2,430

B $2,510

C $2,650

D $3,000

129 Which of the following is a direct expense?

A   Assembly labour required on each unit of production

B   Factory insurance costs

C   Administrative salaries

D   The hire of a special machine required for a particular job

130 A new machine has an estimated five-year life and a nil disposal value at the end of its life. Depreciation methods being considered are:

(i)   reducing balance at 25% per annum

(ii)   straight-line.

Which of the following statements is correct?

A   Depreciation in each year would be greater using the reducing balance method.

B   Depreciation in each year would be greater using the straight-line method.

C   Depreciation would be greater in year 1 but less in year 5 if the reducing balance method, rather than the straight-line method, were used.

D   Depreciation would be greater in year 1 but less in year 5 if the straight-line method, rather than the reducing balance method, were used.

131 Insert a tick to indicate which TWO of the following items will usually be treated as production overhead costs:

	Production overhead costs
Training of direct operatives	
Wages of distribution staff	
Normal idle time in the factory	
Productive time of direct operatives	
Sales personnel salaries.	

132 A fixed asset has an expected life of 10 years with a nil residual value. The asset is due to be depreciated using the straight-line method.

Which of the following statements is correct regarding the use of the reducing balance method instead?

A   Depreciation will be higher in each year using 20% reducing balance

B   Depreciation will be higher in each of years 1, 2 and 3 using 25% reducing balance

C   Depreciation will be lower in each year using 15% reducing balance

D   Depreciation will be lower in year 2 using 18% reducing balance

133   **Select whether the following statements relate to depreciation are true or false:**

	True	False
Using the reducing balance method, product unit costs decline from year to year if output stays the same.		
Using the straight-line method, product unit costs decline as output increases.		

134   **Which of the following relates to capital expenditure?**

  A   Cost of acquiring or enhancing non-current assets

  B   Expenditure on the manufacture of goods or the provision of services

  C   Cost of acquiring stationery for use in the business

  D   Cost of acquiring machinery to be used for resale

Section 3

COSTING TECHNIQUES

ABSORPTION COSTING

135 Which of the following is not normally a reason for determining the absorption cost of a product?

A   To value inventory

B   To help in setting a selling price

C   To determine the difference with marginal costing

D   To help management better understand total costs

136 The process of sharing out overhead costs on a fair basis and the second stage in absorption costing is known as

A   Overhead apportionment

B   Overhead absorption

C   Overhead allocation

D   Overhead costing

137 Which of the following is NOT a reason for using pre-determined overhead absorption rates?

A   Under/over absorption of overheads is avoided

B   It is more useful in setting selling prices in advance

C   It avoids the impact of seasonality in overheads

D   It avoids the impact of any abnormal costs

138 Factory overheads can be absorbed by which of the following methods? *(select all that apply)*

	Acceptable method?
Direct labour hours	
Machine hours	
As a % of prime cost	
$x per unit	

139 The stores overhead in an engineering company for the budget period was $82,100. It is to be re-apportioned on the basis of estimated requisitions to be issued in the period.

The business has four cost centres serviced by the stores cost centre, and data relating to the budget shows:

Cost centre	Estimated requisitions
Machining	6,000
Finishing	6,500
Packing	3,200
Maintenance	1,200

The amount re-apportioned to the Finishing cost centre would be $_____

140 **Absorption costing is concerned with which of the following?**

A   Direct materials

B   Direct labour

C   Fixed costs

D   Variable and fixed costs

141 **A company absorbs production overheads using a machine hour basis. In order to calculate any over or under absorbed overheads which of the following would be needed, in addition to the pre-determined machine hour rate?**

A   Budgeted overheads and actual overheads incurred

B   Budgeted overheads and actual hours worked

C   Actual overheads incurred and budgeted hours

D   Actual overheads incurred and actual hours worked

142 A company has two production departments, Cutting and Finishing.

The budgeted overheads and operating hours for the two departments for the next year are:

Cutting	$210,000	60,000 machine hours	4,000 labour hours
Finishing	$200,000	5,000 machine hours	14,000 labour hours

From the information given, the pre-determined overhead absorption rates for the departments should be based on which basis? *(select one basis for each department)*

	Machine hours	Labour hours
Cutting department		
Finishing department		

143 **What is the term associated with charging a specific item of overhead cost to one particular department?**

A   Absorption

B   Allocation

C   Apportionment

D   Re-apportionment

144 A company budgeted to produce 3,000 units of a single product in a period at a budgeted cost per unit, built up as follows:

	$/unit
Direct costs	12
Variable overhead	5
Fixed overhead	9
	$26

In the period covered by the budget:

(a) Actual sales were 3,500 units and finished inventory decreased by 300 units.

(b) Actual fixed overhead expenditure was 5% above that budgeted – all other costs were as budgeted.

Place a tick to indicate the value of the overheads over/under-absorption in the period:

	$450	$1,450	Under	Over
Absorption of overheads				

145 Canberra has established the following information regarding fixed overheads for the coming month:

Budgeted information

Fixed overheads	$180,000
Labour hours	3,000 hours
Machine hours	10,000 hours
Units of production	5,000 units

Actual fixed costs for the last month were $160,000.

Canberra produces many different products using highly automated manufacturing processes and absorbs overheads on the most appropriate basis.

What will be the pre-determined overhead absorption rate?

A $16

B $18

C $36

D $60

146 Overheads in a production cost centre for a period are:

Budget	$74,600
Absorbed	$71,890
Actual	$73,220

What is the overhead over/under absorption?

A $1,330 over absorbed

B $1,330 under absorbed

C $2,710 over absorbed

D $2,710 under absorbed

147 The management accountant of Gympie has already allocated and apportioned the fixed overheads for the period although she has yet to re-apportion the service centre costs. Information for the period is as follows:

	Production departments		Service departments		Total
	1	2	Stores	Maintenance	
Allocated and apportioned	$17,500	$32,750	$6,300	$8,450	$65,000
Work done by:					
Stores	60%	40%	–	–	
Maintenance	75%	20%	5%	–	

The step-down method is used to re-apportion service centre costs.

The total overheads included in production department 1 will be $_____

148 In a given year a production department incurred actual overheads of $178,000. Overheads are absorbed using actual machine hours and a pre-determined rate per hour. The budgeted overhead for the year was $180,000 and the budgeted machine hours were 90,000. The overheads for the year were over absorbed by $4,000.

The actual machine hours were _____ hours.

149 A company is considering the following methods for apportioning heating and lighting costs to its various departments:

1   The relative floor areas of departments

2   The relative cubic capacity (volume) of departments

3   The relative usage ascertained from meters

Which of the above would be acceptable?

A   Methods 1 and 2 only

B   Methods 1 and 3 only

C   Methods 2 and 3 only

D   Methods 1, 2 and 3

150 A company had the following budgeted and actual production overhead costs in its two production cost centres, Machining and Assembly:

	Budget	Actual
Machining	$210,000	$212,000
Assembly	$136,000	$134,000

Which statement is TRUE?

	Over-absorbed	Under-absorbed	Impossible to determine
Machining department			
Assembly department			

151 **Which of the following would be the most appropriate basis for re-apportioning the cost of personnel services in a factory?**

A Floor space occupied

B Hours worked by direct operatives

C Number of direct operatives

D Number of employees

152 The following production overhead costs relate to a production cost centre:

Budget $124,000

Actual $126,740

Absorbed $125,200

Place a tick to indicate the value of the overheads over/under-absorption in the period:

	$1,200	$1,540	Under	Over
Absorption of overheads				

153 An overhead absorption rate of $12.00 per direct labour hour was established based on a budget of 2,100 hours. Actual direct labour hours worked were 2,180 and actual overhead expenditure was $25,470.

What was the over/under absorption of overhead?

A $270 under absorption

B $690 over absorption

C $960 over absorption

D $960 under absorption

154 Machine hours are used to absorb overheads in a production cost centre. Overheads allocated and apportioned to the cost centre are:

	$
Allocated	13,122
Apportioned	7,920
Re-apportioned from service cost centres	2,988

216,000 units of product are manufactured at a rate of 120 units per machine hour.

The overhead absorption rate per machine hour is $ _____ *(round to two decimal places)*

155 There are two production cost centres and two service cost centres in a factory. Production overheads have been allocated and apportioned to cost centres and now require re-apportionment from service cost centres to production cost centres. Relevant details are:

	Service Centre A	Service Centre B
Total overhead	$42,000	$57,600
% to Production Cost Centre X	40	55
% to Production Cost Centre Y	60	45

The total re-apportionment to Production Cost Centre Y is $_____

156 Overheads are absorbed at a pre-determined rate based on direct labour hours. The following additional information is available for a period:

Budget	$164,000 overhead expenditure;	10,000 direct labour hours
Actual	$158,000 overhead expenditure;	9,800 direct labour hours

What was the overhead over/under absorption in the period?

A $2,720 over absorption

B $3,224 over absorption

C $3,280 under absorption

D $6,000 under absorption

157 Over absorbed overheads occur when:

A   absorbed overheads exceed actual overheads

B   absorbed overheads exceed budgeted overheads

C   actual overheads exceed budgeted overheads

D   budgeted overheads exceed absorbed overheads

158 A company uses absorption costing. In a period, 34,000 units of the company's single product were manufactured and 33,000 units were sold.

Consider the following two statements:

1   Fixed production overheads would be over absorbed.

2   Profit would be higher than in the previous period.

Are the statements true in relation to the situation described or is it not possible to determine whether or not they are true?

	Statement 1	*Statement 2*
A	Cannot determine	Cannot determine
B	Cannot determine	True
C	True	Cannot determine
D	True	True

159 A business uses marginal costing and has created the following standard cost card:

	$
Direct material costs (6 kg × $4)	24
Direct labour costs (2 hours × $40 per hour)	80
	——
Marginal production cost	104
	——

The company wants to switch to an absorption costing system. It has determined that budgeted production is 40,000 units, budgeted fixed production overheads are $800,000 and that overheads should be absorbed on the basis of direct labour hours.

The absorption cost per unit for the product will be $ _____ *(round to two decimal places)*

160 Carrell produces two types of jacket, Blouson and Bomber, in its factory that is divided into two departments, cutting and stitching. The firm wishes to calculate a fixed overhead cost per unit figure from the following budgeted data:

	Cutting dept	*Stitching dept*
Allocated fixed overheads	$120,000	$72,000
Labour hours per unit		
Blouson	0.05 hours	0.20 hours
Bomber	0.10 hours	0.25 hours
Budgeted production		
Blouson	6,000 units	6,000 units
Bomber	6,000 units	6,000 units

Fixed overheads are absorbed by reference to labour hours.

The fixed overhead cost of a Bomber is $_____ *(round to two decimal places)*

161 A management consultancy recovers overheads on chargeable consulting hours. Budgeted overheads were $615,000 and actual consulting hours were 32,150. Overheads were under recovered by $35,000.

If actual overheads were $694,075, the budgeted overhead absorption rate per hour was $____ per hour *(round to two decimal places)*

162 Overheads in a factory are apportioned to four production cost centres (A, B, C and D). Direct labour hours are used to absorb overheads in A and B and machine hours are used in C and D. The following information is available:

	Production cost centre			
	A	*B*	*C*	*D*
Overhead expenditure ($)	18,757	29,025	46,340	42,293
Direct labour hours	3,080	6,750	3,760	2,420
Machine hours	580	1,310	3,380	2,640

Which cost centre has the highest hourly overhead absorption rate?

A Production cost centre A

B Production cost centre B

C Production cost centre C

D Production cost centre D

163 **Which of the following is the most appropriate basis for apportioning the canteen costs in a factory?**

A Direct labour hours

B Direct wages

C Indirect labour hours

D Number of factory employees

164 The following data are available relating to overheads in two production cost centres:

	Cost centre A	Cost centre B
Budget	$54,030	$76,910
Actual	?	?
Absorbed	$54,960	$76,250
Over/under-absorbed	?	$520 under-absorbed

What is known on the basis of the available data above?

A   Actual overheads in cost centre B were less than budget

B   Overheads absorbed in cost centre B exceeded actual overheads

C   Overheads were over-absorbed in cost centre A

D   Overheads were under-absorbed in cost centre A

165 A company sold 56,000 units of its single product in a period for a total revenue of $700,000. Finished inventory increased by 4,000 units in the period. Costs in the period were:

Variable production	$3.60 per unit
Fixed production	$258,000 (absorbed on the actual number of units produced)
Fixed non-production	$144,000

Using absorption costing, what was the profit for the period?

A $82,000

B $96,400

C $113,600

D $123,200

166 A company has two production cost centres (PC1 and PC2) and two service cost centres (SC1 and SC2). Overhead allocation and apportionment is as follows for a period:

	PC1	PC2	SC1	SC2
Overheads	$460,200	$520,800	$122,000	$96,600
Reapportionment of SC1	35%	45%		20%
Reapportionment of SC2	30%	70%		

What are the total overheads in PC2 after reapportionment of the service cost centre overheads?

A $605,500

B $643,320

C $660,400

D $667,720

167 An accountancy practice had an overhead budget of $21,060 for a period. Actual overhead expenditure in the period was $21,720. Overheads are absorbed on the basis of client hours worked which totalled 2,375 in the period and resulted in under-absorption of $345.

The budgeted overhead absorption rate per client hour was $_____ per hour (round to two decimal places)

168 What production overheads are included in product costs using absorption costing? *(select all that apply)*

	Included in product costs?
Direct overhead costs	
Fixed overhead costs	
Variable overhead costs	

169 A company had total revenue of $169,000 in a period from the sale of 6,500 units of its single product. There was no finished goods inventory at the beginning of the period and 200 units were in inventory at the end of the period. Production costs in the period were:

Variable costs $93,130

Fixed costs $41,540

Fixed costs are absorbed on an actual basis using units produced.

The gross profit in the period was $_____

170 Which of the following correctly describes a service centre?

A   A department operating outside the production function but not involved directly in the manufacture of products

B   A department operating within the production function and involved directly in the manufacture of products

C   A department operating outside the production function and involved directly in the manufacture of products

D   A department operating within the production function but not involved directly in the manufacture of products

171 A company has a marginal production cost per unit of $15, based on a standard of 2 labour hours per unit. It uses an absorption costing system, and the following information is available for fixed production costs:

	Budget	Actual
Fixed overhead costs	$60,000	$50,000
Direct labour hours	15,000	10,000

Fixed costs are absorbed on the basis of direct labour hours.

The absorption cost per unit for the product is $_____ *(round to two decimal places)*

172 Which of the following may result from the use of predetermined rates set for a year rather than actual rates recalculated every three months?

	Result from the use of predetermined rates?
Delay in the establishment of job costs	
Change in unit costs reflecting seasonal activity	
Overhead over or under recovery	

MARGINAL COSTING

173 When preparing an income statement based on marginal costing principles, inventory valuation comprises which of the following costs?

   A   Direct labour and material only

   B   Prime cost plus production overhead

   C   Prime cost plus variable overhead

   D   Total cost of sales

174 A company has put together a standard cost card for its single product as shown below. Budgeted monthly production is 2,500 units.

	$
Selling price	150
Direct labour (5 hours @ $10/hour)	-50
Direct materials (6 litres @ $5/litre)	30
Variable overhead (5 hours @ $6 hour)	30
Fixed overhead	15
Profit	25

The activity level in December was not the same as budgeted and the data from the cost card was used to recalculate the budgeted profit for the actual activity level using a marginal costing system. The flexed budget showed a profit of $54,500.

Actual costs in December were as budgeted except for materials which were 20% more expensive and variable overheads which were 30% cheaper.

Using a marginal costing system the actual profit for December would be $_____

175 33,300 units of a product were manufactured in a period during which 33,950 units were sold for a total revenue of $1,391,950. Opening inventory of the product was 1,700 units. The company uses absorption costing. Unit costs of the product were:

Variable manufacturing costs $16.30

Fixed manufacturing costs $11.60

Variable selling and administration costs $3.40

Fixed selling and administration costs $7.10

What was the change in the value of finished goods inventory over the period?

   A $10,595

   B $18,135

   C $24,960

   D $29,295

176 In a month, Z Co has budgeted sales of 15,000 units and budgeted production of 17,000 units.

The profit under marginal costing is $10,000 lower than when profit is calculated under absorption costing.

The fixed production overhead cost per unit was $_____

177 Total contribution is calculated by which formula?

A Total revenue less total costs

B Total revenue less variable costs

C Total revenue less fixed costs

D Total revenue less production costs

The following information relates to questions 178 and 179.

Dundee makes cakes, for which the budgeted profit per unit is as follows:

	$
Materials	2
Labour	3
Variable production overhead	3
Fixed production overhead	4
Variable selling cost	1
Fixed selling overhead	2
Profit	5
	___
Sales price	20
	___

Both types of fixed overheads were based on a budget of 10,000 cakes a year.

In the first year of production, the only difference from the budget was that Dundee produced 11,000 cakes and sold 9,000. All costs and revenues were in line with the levels budgeted per unit.

178 The profit made under an absorption costing system was $_____

179 The profit using a marginal costing system was $_____

180 A company currently uses absorption costing. The following information relates to Product X for Month 1:

Opening inventory Nil

Production 900 units

Sales 800 units

If the company had used marginal costing, what would happen to profit and inventory value?

	Higher	Lower
Profit		
Inventory value		

181 A company uses marginal costing. In valuing inventory of finished goods which of the following would NOT be included in the valuation?

A Machine operator's wages

B Factory rent

C Royalty fees per unit

D Raw materials

182 A company manufactures a single product. Production and sales quantities for a period were:

	Production	Sales
Budget	100,000 units	102,000 units
Actual	97,000 units	96,000 units

The fixed production overhead absorption rate is $1.40 per unit.

If marginal costing had been used instead of absorption costing how would the profit for the period have differed?

A $1,400 less using marginal costing

B $1,400 more using marginal costing

C $4,200 less using marginal costing

D $4,200 more using marginal costing

183 A company sold 82,000 units of its single product in a period in which 84,000 units were manufactured.

Are the following statements true or false?

	True	False
Inventory value at the end of the period would be higher than at the beginning of the period.		
Inventory values both at the beginning and at the end of the period would be higher using absorption rather than marginal costing.		

184 **Which TWO of the following statements are true?**

	True
In a marginal costing profit statement, variable selling costs are deducted before contribution is calculated	
In an absorption costing profit statement, all fixed costs are shown together	
Absorption costing treats total fixed costs as period costs	
Examining contribution per unit is a better way to determine the impact on profit of a change in sales volume than examining profit per unit	

185 A company has the following standard cost card for its product:

	$
Selling price	60
Variable costs	20
Fixed costs	10
	—
Profit	30
	—

The fixed costs are based on a budgeted level of sales and volume of 6,000 units.

The company plans to increase its selling price by $10. This will have the effect of changing volume to 5,000 units and variable costs to $18 per unit.

The change will increase expected profit by $_____

186 What distinguishes absorption costing from marginal costing?

  A Product costs include both prime cost and production overhead

  B Product costs include both production and non-production costs

  C Inventory valuation includes a share of all production costs

  D Inventory valuation includes a share of all costs

187 A company uses a marginal costing system. 10,000 units of its single product were manufactured in a period during which 9,760 units were sold.

  If absorption costing is applied instead, what would be the effect on profit?

  A Higher by (240 units × Fixed production overhead cost per unit)

  B Lower by (240 units × Fixed production overhead cost per unit)

  C Higher by [240 units × (Fixed production overhead cost per unit + Fixed non-production overhead cost per unit)]

  D Lower by [240 units × (Fixed production overhead cost per unit + Fixed non-production overhead cost per unit)]

188 A company with a single product sells more units than it manufactures in a period.

  Which of the following correctly describes the use of marginal costing in comparison with absorption costing in the above situation?

  A Both profit and inventory values will be higher

  B Both profit and inventory values will be lower

  C Profit will be higher; inventory values will be lower

  D Profit will be lower; inventory values will be higher

189 A company, which manufactures and sells a single product, has the following sales and production data for a period:

  Production   2,200 units

  Sales   2,000 units

  Contribution per unit is $5.

  Fixed overheads per unit are $10.

  What is the value of the absorption and marginal costing profits for the business?

	$10,000	$11,200	$11,500	$12,000
Absorption costing profit				
Marginal costing profit				

190 Are the following statements about marginal costing TRUE or FALSE?

	True	False
Inventory value will always be lower than when using absorption costing		
Profit will always be higher than when using absorption costing		

191 A company, which uses marginal costing, normally manufactures 1,000 units of a product in a period. The product is sold for $50 per unit. Costs for the 1,000 units are:

Direct materials	$16,300
Direct labour	$9,800
Fixed overheads	$21,600

How much profit will be expected if 1,100 units of the product are manufactured and sold in a period?

A $2,300

B $2,530

C $4,690

D $7,300

192 A company manufactures and sells 4,000 units of a product each month at a selling price of $22 per unit. The prime cost of the product is $11.60 per unit and the monthly overheads are:

	$
Variable production	7,200
Variable selling and administration	5,200
Fixed production	16,400
Fixed selling and administration	6,800

What is the product's gross profit margin (to one decimal place)?

A   6.8%

B   20.5%

C   33.2%

D   59.5%

193 A product has the following costs:

	$/unit
Variable production costs	4.80
Total production costs	7.50
Total variable costs	5.90
Total costs	10.00

11,400 units of the product were manufactured in a period during which 11,200 units were sold.

What is the profit difference using absorption costing rather than marginal costing?

A   The profit for the period is $540 lower

B   The profit for the period is $540 higher

C   The profit for the period is $820 lower

D   The profit for the period is $820 higher

JOB AND BATCH COSTING

194   **Which of the following businesses would operate a batch costing system?**

   A   Brewery

   B   Food canning

   C   Coal mine

   D   Bakery

195   **Which of the following would operate a job costing system?**

   A   Shipbuilder

   B   Oil refinery

   C   Steel producer

   D   Kitchen fitter

196   **Bay Agricultural Engineers is preparing a quote for Job 731. The costs and other related information includes:**

	$
Raw materials	4,250
Direct labour	7,200
Production overhead	$5.50 per labour hour
Administrative overhead	10% of production cost
Profit margin	25% of selling price

   Note: Direct labour is paid $7.20 per hour.

   The sales price of Job 731 to the customer would have been $_____ (round to the nearest $)

197   **Job costing will normally be used where:**

   A   a given number of similar products are produced

   B   production is continuous

   C   production of the product takes an extensive period of time

   D   production relates to a single special order

198   A small engineering company that makes generators specifically to customers' own designs has had to purchase some special tools for a particular job. The tools will have no further use after the work has been completed and will be scrapped.

   The cost of these tools should be treated as:

   A   variable production overheads

   B   fixed production overheads

   C   indirect expenses

   D   direct expenses

199   A firm of accountants conducts a number of audits for local companies each year.

   Which of the following costing methods would it use?

   A   Process costing

   B   Service costing

   C   Job costing

   D   Batch costing

200   Job XX has been completed at a total production cost of $3,633. Administration and selling overheads are applied at 20% of production cost. The selling price of each job is established so as to provide a GROSS profit margin of 30%.

   The selling price of Job XX is $_____ *(round to the nearest $)*

201   A jobbing enterprise calculates the prices of its jobs by adding overheads to the prime cost and adding 30% to total costs as a profit margin. Job number 256 was sold for $1,690 and incurred overheads of $694. What was the prime cost of the job?

   A $489

   B $507

   C $606

   D $996

202   **Which THREE of the costs listed below are contained in a typical job cost?**

	Part of job costs?
Actual direct material cost	
Actual direct labour cost	
Actual manufacturing overheads	
Absorbed manufacturing overheads	

203   Costs for Job 123 are:

   Direct materials $460

   Direct labour $600

   Overheads   120% of direct labour cost

   A profit margin of 20% of selling price is required.

   The selling price of Job 123 was $_____ *(round to the nearest $)*

204   A job cost estimate includes 630 productive labour hours. In addition, it is anticipated that idle time will be 10% of the total hours paid for the job. The wage rate is $12 per hour.

   What is the total estimated labour cost for the job?

   A $6,804

   B $7,560

   C $8,316

   D $8,400

205 In a factory operating job costing which of the following costs will be overheads allocated to individual cost centres?

	Overheads?
Salaries of supervisors, each of whom are responsible for two cost centres, where no record is kept of their time in each cost centre	
Wages of skilled operators assigned to individual jobs, in particular cost centres, with time recorded on time sheets	
Wages of labourers who are moved from cost centre to cost centre and who maintain detailed time sheets. They are not assigned to work on specific orders in each cost centre.	

206 In which of the following manufacturing environments would job costing be appropriate?

1   Production is carried out in accordance with the special requirements of each customer

2   Products are mass produced for inventory

3   Joint products are manufactured

A   1 only

B   1 and 2

C   3 only

D   2 and 3

207 Consider whether the following statements are TRUE or FALSE?

	True	False
Cost control in job costing is less important than in traditional costing		
Cost control in batch costing is less important than in traditional costing		

208 A construction company employs a job costing system, which of the following will be helpful in ensuring strong cost control measures?

	Strong cost control
Timesheets are completed and examined at the end of the job	
The client is charged a mark-up on actual job costs	
Materials requisitions are approved by a job supervisor	
Regular checkpoints are implemented for examining cost-to-date	

PROCESS COSTING

The following data relates to questions 209 and 210.

Pickersons manufactures a series of cleaning materials which pass through separate processes. The input to Process A for the month of January was:

Material Z   10,000 tonnes at $3.00 per tonne

Direct labour $6,500

Process overheads $11,500

Normal losses are estimated as 5% of input and all losses have a scrap value of $2.00 per tonne.

Output during the month to Process B was 9,450 tonnes and there is no work-in-progress.

209 **What was the value of normal losses credited to the process account in January?**

   A $500

   B $750

   C $1,250

   D $1,000

210 **The number of tonnes accounted for as abnormal losses or abnormal gains in the month were _____ tonnes**

211 A company operates a continuous process into which it inputs 30,000 tonnes of material costing $6 per tonne. It also incurs direct labour costs of $25,000 and process overheads of $145,000.

   Normal losses are estimated at 10% of input and all losses have a scrap value of $3 per tonne.

   What is the cost per unit of output?

   A $12.63

   B $11.67

   C $12.96

   D $11.37

212 **In which circumstances would a normal loss be given a value or cost of nil?**

   A   If an abnormal loss also exists

   B   If an abnormal gain also exists

   C   If the scrap value is excessively high

   D   If it has no scrap value

213 Burgess operates a continuous process into which 3,000 units of material costing $9,000 was input in a period.

Conversion costs for this period were $11,970 and losses, which have a scrap value of $1.50 per unit, are expected at a rate of 10% of input. There was no opening or closing inventory and output for the period was 2,900 units.

The valuation of the output was $_____ *(round to the nearest $)*

214 Products A and B are manufactured in a joint process. The following data is available for a period:

Joint process cost		$30,000
Output:	Product A	2,000 kg
	Product B	4,000 kg
Selling price:	Product A	$12 per kg
	Product B	$18 per kg

What is Product B's share of the joint process costs if the sales value method of cost apportionment is used?

A $7,500

B $18,000

C $20,000

D $22,500

215 Perth operates a process costing system. The process is expected to lose 25% of input and this can be sold for $8 per kg.

Inputs for the month were:

Direct materials	3,500 kg at a total cost of $52,500
Direct labour	$9,625 for the period

There is no opening or closing work-in-progress in the period. Actual output was 2,800 kg.

What is the valuation of the output?

A $44,100

B $49,700

C $58,800

D $56,525

216 A company discovers, at the end of a process, that abnormal losses had occurred.

At what value would a unit of abnormal loss be recorded in the process account?

A The total cost per unit of normal output

B Scrap value

C The direct cost per unit of normal output

D Nil value

217 The total production cost of joint products can be apportioned between these products using which THREE of the following methods?

	Used to apportion joint costs?
Weight	
Sales revenue	
Selling prices	
Net realisable value	

218 A company input 500 kilos of material into a process at a cost of $7,000. As expected it had to scrap 10% of the input and it sold this for $10 per kilo.

What was the net material cost (to the nearest penny) per kilo of good production?

A $13.00

B $14.00

C $14.44

D $15.56

219 How should the cost of disposing of normal waste arising in a process be treated, if the waste has no saleable value?

A   Debited to the process account

B   Credited to the process account

C   Debited to the normal loss account

D   Credited to the normal loss account

220 6,500 kg of a product were manufactured in a period. There is a normal loss of 20% of the weight of material input.

An abnormal gain of 4% of the material input occurred in the period.

The amount of material input to production in the period was _____ kgs *(to the nearest kg)*

221 How are abnormal GAINS recorded in a process account?

A   Credited at a cost per unit based on total production cost divided by actual output

B   Credited at a cost per unit based on total production cost divided by normal output

C   Debited at a cost per unit based on total production cost divided by actual output

D   Debited at a cost per unit based on total production cost divided by normal output

222 Are the following statements relating to process costing true or false?

	True	False
The higher the net realisable value of normal losses the lower will be the cost per unit of normal output.		
The higher the abnormal losses the higher will be the cost per unit of normal output.		

223 4,000 litres of a chemical were manufactured in a period. There is a normal loss of 6% of the material input to the manufacturing process. There was an abnormal loss of 4% of the material input in the period.

How many litres of material (to the nearest litre) were input during the period?

A   3,600

B   4,255

C   4,400

D   4,444

224 The value of cost and profit data using joint product costing is often questioned when pre-separation costs make up a very high proportion of the total production cost of a joint product.

In which of the following circumstances would this problem be overcome?

A   The use of arbitrary allocation in the apportionment of joint costs

B   Identifying and removing loss making joint products

C   Monitoring total profits for all of the joint products together rather than individually

D   Using the net realisable value method of joint product cost apportionment

225 Charleville operates a continuous process producing three products and one by-product. Output from the process for a month was as follows:

Product	Selling price per unit	Units of output from process
1	$18	10,000
2	$25	20,000
3	$20	20,000
4 (by-product)	$2	3,500

Total output costs were $277,000.

What was the unit valuation for Product 3 using the sales revenue basis for allocating joint costs?

A $4.70

B $4.80

C $5.00

D $5.10

226 12,000 kg of a material were input to a process in a period. The normal loss is 10% of input. There is no opening or closing work-in-progress. Output in the period was 10,920 kg.

What was the abnormal gain/loss in the period?

A   Abnormal gain of 120 kg

B   Abnormal loss of 120 kg

C   Abnormal gain of 1,080 kg

D   Abnormal loss of 1,080 kg

227 Are the following statements relating to joint product costing true or false?

	True	False
In costing for joint products, apportioning joint costs using net realisable values will always result in higher costs being apportioned to each product than using volume of output.		
The benefit of further processing should be evaluated on the basis of incremental costs and revenues only.		

228 Costs incurred in a process totalled $216,720 for a period. 24,000 units of finished product were manufactured including 1,200 units which were rejected on inspection and disposed of. The level of rejects in the period was normal. Rejects are sold for $2.00 per unit.

What was the cost per unit for the process?

A $8.93

B $9.03

C $9.40

D $9.51

229 Are the following statements relating to joint product cost apportionment true or false?

	True	False
Using the sales value method of cost apportionment, and where there is no further processing, the gross profit margin of each product will be the same.		
Using the units of output method of cost apportionment, the joint cost per unit will be the same for all joint products.		

230 Which of the following correctly describes a by-product?

A A product with a significant sales value that is produced in the same process as joint products

B A product with an insignificant sales value that is produced in the same process as joint products

C A product with a significant sales value that is produced in a different process to joint products

D A product with an insignificant sales value that is produced in a different process to joint products

SERVICE COSTING

231 Which of the following is not a cost unit associated with service costing?

A   Out-patient day

B   Passenger mile

C   Guest day

D   Tonne of stone quarried

232 XY Taxis runs a fleet of vehicles. Vehicle M9 DUN is part of the fleet and its budget for Year 20X5 is:

Drivers' wages	$13,500
Fuel	$8,500
Maintenance	$750
Tax and insurance	$1,000

Depreciation: 25% reducing balance method. The vehicle had been purchased for $16,000 in Year 20X3.

Planned kilometres to be travelled: 50,000 per annum.

What were the total budgeted operating costs for the year?

A $27,750

B $25,000

C $26,000

D $23,750

233 Which of the following cost classifications is used in service costing:

A   Maintenance expenses

B   Fixed expenses

C   Operating and running expenses

D   All of the above

234 Which of the following is not typically a feature of service costing?

	Not applicable to service costing
Allocating costs between fixed and variable elements	
Unique nature of the work	
Accurate time recording	
Work that extends beyond one accounting period	
Accuracy in valuing work in progress	

235 When is service costing used?

A   When indirect costs are a small proportion of total costs

B   When overhead absorption is straightforward

C   When the absence of a physical product makes it impossible to determine unit costs

D   When the output is intangible

236 The cost unit of a transport business with a single vehicle is tonne/kilometre. Total costs were $4,558 in a week during which the following journeys were made:

Journey	Load (tonnes)	Distance (kms)
1	5	80
2	7	100
3	3	40
4	5	60
5	4	150

The cost per tonne/kilometre in the week was $_____ *(round to the nearest $)*

237 In a 30-day period a restaurant was open for 9 hours per day. Costs incurred in the period totalled $65,124. The following additional information is available:

Number of tables available	15
Number of seats per table	4
Customer turnround	1 hour
Seating occupancy achieved	60%

The cost per customer was $_____ *(round to the nearest $)*

Section 4

DECISION-MAKING

COST/VOLUME/PROFIT ANALYSIS

238 A company has put together the following budget based on production and sales of 5,000 units

	$
Sales	45,000
Cost of sales	(29,000)
Gross profit	16,000
Administration costs	(12,000)
Net profit	4,000

The following information is also available:

The variable production cost per unit is budgeted to be $5.

Administration costs include a $2 per unit selling cost with the remainder representing fixed administration overhead.

What is the margin of safety in percentage terms?

A   30%

B   120%

C   167%

D   40%

239 GG manufactures a product that has a selling price of $15 and a variable cost of $6 per unit. Annual fixed costs are $43,875 and annual sales demand is 6,000 units.

New manufacturing methods are being considered for the product. These would result in a rise of 20% in fixed costs and a reduction in the variable cost per unit to $5. The new manufacturing methods would create a higher quality product and sales demand would increase to 7,000 units each year at a higher sales price of $20 per unit.

If the changes in manufacturing methods are implemented, and if the selling price is raised to $20, the break-even level would be:

A   975 units higher

B   1,365 units higher

C   1,950 units lower

D   1,365 units lower

240 If both the selling price per unit and variable cost per unit of a company rise by 10%, the break-even point will:

A   remain constant

B   increase

C   fall

D   be impossible to determine without further information

241 The budgeted cost of the only type of product made in the factory of SD, based on an expected monthly level of production and sales of 1,000 is as follows:

	$
Variable production costs	5.60
Fixed production costs	5.80
Variable selling costs	3.40
Fixed selling costs	4.60
Profit	5.50
Selling price	$24.90

The break-even point is:

A   365 units

B   513 units

C   654 units

D   920 units

242 AL makes a single product which it sells for $10 per unit. Fixed costs are $48,000 per month and the product has a contribution to sales ratio of 40%.

In a period when actual sales were $140,000, AL's margin of safety, in units, was _____

243 The following information relates to Product P:

	$ per unit
Selling price	65
Direct materials cost	22
Direct labour cost	14
Variable production overhead cost	9
Fixed production overhead cost	10

Budgeted output of Product P for the year is 12,000 units.

Assuming that no inventory of Product P is held, what number of units must be made and sold to make a profit of $18,000 in the year?

A   4,759 units

B   6,000 units

C   6,900 units

D   13,800 units

244 Dane makes and sells a single product which has a selling price of $26, prime costs are $10 and overheads (all fixed) are absorbed at 50% of prime cost. Fixed overheads are $50,000.

The break-even point (to the nearest whole unit) is _____ units

245 A company has established the following information for the costs and revenues at an activity level of 500 units:

	$
Direct materials	2,500
Direct labour	5,000
Production overheads	1,000
Selling costs	1,250
Total cost	9,750
Sales revenue	17,500
Profit	7,750

20% of the selling costs and 50% of the production overheads are fixed over all levels of activity.

The profit at an activity level of 1,000 units would be $_____

246 A company has calculated its margin of safety as 20% on budgeted sales and budgeted sales are 5,000 units per month.

What would be the budgeted fixed costs if the budgeted contribution was $25 per unit?

A $100,000

B $125,000

C $150,000

D $160,000

247 Which of the following describes the margin of safety?

A   Actual contribution margin achieved compared with that required to break even

B   Actual sales compared with sales required to break even

C   Actual versus budgeted net profit margin

D   Actual versus budgeted sales

248 E plc operates a marginal costing system. For the forthcoming year, variable costs are budgeted to be 60% of sales value and fixed costs are budgeted to be 30% of sales value.

If E plc increases its selling prices by 10%, and if fixed costs, variable costs per unit and sales volume remain unchanged, the effect on E plc's contribution would be:

A   a decrease of 6%

B   an increase of 10%

C   an increase of 25%

D   an increase of 100%

249 A company has established a budgeted sales revenue for the forthcoming period of $500,000 with an associated contribution of $275,000. Fixed production costs are $137,500 and fixed selling costs are $27,500.

The break-even sales revenue is $_____

The following information relates to questions 250 and 251.

Sales units	128,000
Sales revenue	$640,000
Variable costs	$384,000
Fixed costs	$210,000

250 What sales revenue is required to earn a profit of $65,000?

A $458,333

B $590,000

C $687,500

D $705,000

251 How many sales units are required to earn a profit of $52,000?

A 52,400 units

B 87,333 units

C 131,000 units

D 160,500 units

252 The following data relates to a company with a single product:

Selling price	$12.50 per unit
Fixed production costs	$77,000 per period
Fixed non-production costs	$46,000 per period
Break-even sales per period	24,600 units

What is the contribution per unit?

A $3.13

B $5.00

C $7.50

D $9.37

253 **What will be the effect on the margin of safety if unit variable costs and total fixed costs both increase, assuming no change in selling price or sales volume?**

A Decrease

B Increase

C Stay the same

D Impossible to determine without more information

The following information relates to questions 254 and 255.

The following planned results are available for a company with a single product:

Sales units	112,000
Sales revenue	$100,800
Variable costs	$60,480
Fixed costs	$36,000

254 What sales revenue is required to earn a profit of $5,000?

    A $68,333

    B $90,000

    C $102,500

    D $113,889

255 The margin of safety (sales units) is _____ units

256 An organisation currently produces one product. The cost per unit of that product is as follows:

	$
Selling price	130
Direct materials	22
Direct labour	15
Direct expenses	3
Variable overheads	10
Total cost	50

Total fixed costs for the period amount to $1,600,000. How many units (to the nearest whole unit) will the organisation need to produce and sell to generate a profit of $250,000?

    A   20,000

    B   20,555

    C   23,125

    D   26,428

257 A product has the following unit costs:

Variable manufacturing	$7.60
Variable non-manufacturing	$1.40
Fixed manufacturing	$3.70
Fixed non-manufacturing	$2.70
The selling price of the product is	$17.50 per unit

The contribution/sales ratio is _____ % *(round to one decimal place)*

258 A company has a single product. The following budgeted information relates to a period:

Sales units	800,000
Sales revenue	$1,000,000
Total variable costs	$590,000
Total fixed costs	$350,000

The sales revenue (to the nearest $000) is required to break even is $_____

259 At the end of a production process a company has 10,000 units of Product Y which can be sold for $4 per unit. However if it is further processed at a cost of $7 per unit it can be sold for $13 per unit.

The net benefit to the company from further processing Product Y is $_____

SHORT-TERM DECISION-MAKING

260 Worth produces four products L, E, W and S which have the following costs per unit:

	L	E	W	S
	$	$	$	$
Direct materials (at $10/kg)	15	10	12.50	20
Direct labour (at $12/hour)	12	12	18.00	18
Overheads (at $6 /labour hour)	12	6	9.00	9
Total cost	39	28	39.50	47
Contribution/unit	10	15	12.00	20
Maximum demand per month	3,000	2,000	1,500	2,500

Only 15,000 kg of materials and 10,250 labour hours are available.

In order to maximise profits, the product that Worth would prefer to produce first is product ___

261 A company manufactures three products (X, Y and Z), all of which pass through the same finishing process. For the coming month the number of hours available in the finishing process is 6,000.

Data relating to each product are as follows:

Product	X	Y	Z
Selling price per unit ($)	30	36	41
Variable cost per unit ($)	20	27	35
Minutes in the finishing process per unit	45	36	25
Maximum monthly demand (units)	4,500	4,500	4,500

Place a tick to indicate the ranking of the products for production given that the company wishes to maximise contribution

	1st	2nd	3rd
X			
Y			
Z			

262 The costs most relevant to be used in decision making are:

A   sunk costs

B   current costs

C   estimated future costs

D   notional and full costs

263 A firm has some material which originally cost $45,000. It has a scrap value of $12,500 but if reworked at a cost of $7,500, it could be sold for $17,500.

The incremental effect of reworking and selling the material would be a loss of $_____

264 In order to utilise some spare capacity, Zola is preparing a quotation for a special order which requires 1,000 kilograms of Material R.

Zola has 600 kilograms of Material R in inventory (original cost $5.00 per kg). Material R is used in the company's main product Q.

The resale value of Material R is $4.00 per kg. The present replacement price of Material R is $6.00. Material R is readily available on the market.

The relevant cost of the 1,000 kilograms of Material R to be included in the quotation is:

A $4,000

B $5,000

C $5,400

D $6,000

265 **Which TWO of the following are NOT normally included in relevant cost decision making?**

	Not relevant?
Future costs	
Committed costs	
Sunk costs	
Incremental variable costs	
Incremental fixed costs	

266 **A sunk cost is:**

A   a cost committed to be spent in the current period

B   a cost that is irrelevant for decision making

C   a cost connected with oil exploration in the North Sea

D   a cost unaffected by fluctuations in the level of activity

267 For decision-making purposes, which of the following are relevant costs? (select all that apply)

	Relevant?
Avoidable cost	
Future cost	
Opportunity cost	
Differential cost	

268 The labour requirements for a special contract are 250 skilled labour hours paid $10 per hour and 750 semi-skilled labour hours paid $8 per hour.

At present skilled labour is in short supply, and all such labour used on this contract will be at the expense of other work which generates $12 contribution per hour (after charging labour costs). There is currently a surfeit of 1,200 semi-skilled labour hours, but the firm temporarily has a policy of no redundancies.

The relevant cost of labour for the special contract is:

A $3,000

B $5,500

C $8,500

D $11,500

269 A company is considering accepting a one-year contract that will require four skilled employees.

The four skilled employees could be recruited on a one-year contract at a cost of $40,000 per employee. The employees would be supervised by an existing manager who earns $60,000 per annum. It is expected that supervision of the contract would take 10% of the manager's time.

Instead of recruiting new employees, the company could retrain some existing employees who currently earn $30,000 per year. The training would cost $15,000 in total. If these employees were used they would need to be replaced at a total cost of $100,000.

The relevant labour cost of the contract is $_____

270 A company produces three products which have the following details:

		Product		
		I	*II*	*III*
		Per unit	*Per unit*	*Per unit*
Direct materials	(at $5/kg)	8 kg	5 kg	6 kg
Contribution per unit		$35	$25	$48
Contribution per kg of material		$4.375	$5	$8
Demand (excluding special contract)	(units)	3,000	5,000	2,000

The company must produce 1,000 units of Product I for a special contract before meeting normal demand.

Unfortunately there are only 35,000 kg of material available.

What is the optimal production plan?

	Product		
	I	*II*	*III*
A	1,000	4,600	2,000
B	1,000	3,000	2,000
C	2,875	–	2,000
D	3,000	2,200	–

271 GR manufactures two products for which details are shown below:

Product	X	Y
Selling price per unit	$66	$100
Variable cost per unit	$42	$75
Fixed cost per unit	$30	$34
Skilled labour per unit	0.40 hours	0.50 hours
Maximum quarterly demand	5,000	5,000

For the current period, GR is experiencing a shortage of skilled labour, of which only 1,000 hours will be available. If products are not produced internally they can be bought in at prices of $50 for X and $80 for Y.

How many units of Product Y should be produced in the period?

A   0 units

B   500 units

C   2,000 units

D   2,500 units

272 You are currently working as an accountant in an insurance company, but you are thinking of starting up your own business. In considering whether or not to start your own business, your current salary would be:

A   a sunk cost

B   an incremental cost

C   an irrelevant cost

D   an opportunity cost

273 What term is used to represent the benefit sacrificed when one course of action is chosen in preference to an alternative?

A   Avoidable cost

B   Direct cost

C   Incremental cost

D   Opportunity cost

274 A company is considering the use of Material X in a special order. A sufficient quantity of the material, which is used regularly by the company in its normal business, is available from inventory.

What is the relevant cost per kg of Material X in the evaluation of the special order?

A   Cost of the last purchase

B   Nil

C   Replacement cost

D   Saleable value

275 A company manufactures and sells four products. Sales demand cannot be met owing to a shortage of skilled labour.

Details of the four products are:

	Product A	Product B	Product C	Product D
Sales demands (units)	1,500	2,000	1,800	1,900
Contribution ($/units)	2.80	2.60	1.90	2.40
Contribution/sales %	30	40	50	45
Skilled labour (hours/units)	1.4	1.2	0.9	1.0

Rank the products in the order in which each should be made in order to maximise profits:

Product	Rank
A	
B	
C	
D	

The following information is relevant to questions 276 and 277.

A special contract requires 100 hours of skilled labour, 200 hours of unskilled labour and 20 hours of management time. Skilled workers are in short supply and would have to be moved from work which is currently earning a contribution of $3.50 per hour. Skilled workers are paid $9 per hour and semi-skilled workers are paid $5 per hour. Management salaries are regarded as fixed costs in the company.

The contract would also require 100 kg of Material N and 300 kg of Material T. Material N is in constant use in the business and there is currently 200 kg of this material held in inventory which is valued at $600. The cost of replacing N is $4 per kg. Material T has no other use in the business. There are currently 200 kg in inventory which could be sold at a value of $4 per kg. The replacement cost of T is $8 per kg.

---

276 What is the relevant cost of labour?

A $1,350

B $2,250

C $2,600

D $2,650

277 The relevant cost of materials is $_____

278 A company currently produces and sells two products, A and B. Details- per unit are as follows:

	A	B
	$	$
Selling price	16	20
Raw material cost	(6)	(8)
Direct labour	(4)	(4)
Fixed cost apportionment	(2)	(4)
Profit per unit	$4	$4

If one of the resources is in short supply and B is preferred to A as a result, the resource in short supply is:

A   impossible to determine

B   raw materials

C   direct labour

D   fixed costs

279 A company manufactures and sells four types of component. The labour hours available for manufacture are restricted but any quantities of the components can be bought-in from an outside supplier in order to satisfy sales demand. The following further information is provided:

	Component			
	A	**B**	**C**	**D**
	Per unit	**Per unit**	**Per unit**	**Per unit**
Selling price ($)	12.00	15.00	18.00	20.00
Variable manufacturing costs ($)	6.00	8.00	9.00	11.50
Bought-in price ($)	11.00	11.50	13.00	16.00
Labour (hours)	0.8	0.8	0.8	0.8

The best component to BUY-IN in order to maximise profit is Component ___

PRINCIPLES OF DISCOUNTED CASH FLOW

280 **If the cost of capital is 8%, the present value of a stream of five annual revenues of $1,000, the first one due now, is closest to:**

A $3,312

B $3,993

C $4,312

D $4,993

Cumulative discount factor at 8%, years 1 – 4 = 3.312

Cumulative discount factor at 8%, years 1 – 5 = 3.993

281 The present value of a five-year annuity which begins in one year's time is $60,000 at a cost of capital of 5% per annum. What is the amount of the annuity?

A $11,259

B $12,000

C $13,860

D $259,740

Cumulative discount factor at 5%, years 1 – 5 = 4.329

282 A company has arranged a ten-year lease at an annual rental of $8,000. The first rental payment has to be made immediately (i.e. in advance) and the others are to be paid at the start of each succeeding year.

The present value of the lease at a discount rate of 12% per annum is $_____ *(round to the nearest $)*

Cumulative discount factor at 12% for years 1 to 9 = 5.328

Cumulative discount factor at 12% for years 1 to 10 = 5.650

283 An individual is to receive an annuity of $5,000 for ten years, at the end of each year. The present value of the annuities is $33,550. What is the cost of capital (r)?

A   2% per annum

B   4% per annum

C   8% per annum

D   16% per annum

284 Dalby is currently considering an investment that gives a positive net present value of $3,664 at 15%. At a discount rate of 20% it has a negative net present value of $21,451.

What is the internal rate of return of this investment?

A   15.7%

B   16.0%

C   19.3%

D   19.9%

285 A capital investment project has an initial investment followed by constant annual returns.

How is the payback period calculated?

A   Initial investment ÷ Annual profit

B   Initial investment ÷ Annual net cash inflow

C   (Initial investment – Residual value) ÷ Annual profit

D   (Initial investment – Residual value) ÷ Annual net cash inflow

286 **Which of the following accurately defines the internal rate of return (IRR)?**

A   The average annual profit from an investment expressed as a percentage of the investment sum

B   The discount rate (%) at which the net present value of the cash flows from an investment is zero

C   The net present value of the cash flows from an investment discounted at the required rate of return

D   The rate (%) at which discounted net profits from an investment are zero

287 A company has a loan of $60,000 and will pay interest on the loan of 10% per annum in perpetuity. The company has a cost of capital of 5%.

The present value of the interest on the loan is $_____

288 An investment project has the following discounted cash flows ($000):

Year		Discount rate	
	0%	10%	20%
0	(90)	(90)	(90)
1	30	27.3	25.0
2	30	24.8	20.8
3	30	22.5	17.4
4	30	20.5	14.5
	30	5.1	(12.3)

The required rate of return on investment is 10% per annum.

What is the discounted payback period of the investment project?

A   Less than 3.0 years

B   3.0 years

C   Between 3.0 years and 4.0 years

D   More than 4.0 years

289 A machine has an investment cost of $60,000 at time 0. The present values (at time 0) of the expected net cash inflows from the machine over its useful life are:

Discount rate	Present value of cash inflows
10%	$64,600
15%	$58,200
20%	$52,100

What is the internal rate of return (IRR) of the machine investment?

A   Below 10%

B   Between 10% and 15%

C   Between 15% and 20%

D   Over 20%

290 An investment project has a positive net present value (NPV) of $7,222 when its cash flows are discounted at the cost of capital of 10% per annum. Net cash inflows from the project are expected to be $18,000 per annum for five years. The cumulative discount (annuity) factor for five years at 10% is 3.791.

The investment at the start of the project is $_____ *(round to the nearest $)*

291 **Which of TWO of the following statements relating to an investment project that has been discounted at rates of 10% and 20 are true:**

	True
The discounted payback period at 10% will be longer than the discounted payback period at 20%.	
The discounted payback period at 20% will be longer than the discounted payback period- at 10%.	
The non-discounted payback period will be longer than the discounted payback period.	
The non-discounted payback period will be shorter than the discounted payback period.	

292 **The effective annual rate of interest of 2.1% compounded every three months is _____ %** *(round to two decimal places)*

293 A company is considering an immediate investment in new machinery. The machinery would cost $100,000 with expected net cash inflows of $30,000 per year starting in Year 1. The disposal value of the machine after five years is expected to be $10,000. $15,000 has already been incurred on development costs.

What is the payback period of the investment based on future incremental cash flows?

A   3.0 years

B   3.3 years

C   3.5 years

D   3.8 years

294 An investment project has net present values as follows:

At a discount rate of 5%	$69,700 positive
At a discount rate of 14%	$16,000 positive
At a discount rate of 20%	$10,500 negative

Using the above figures, what is the BEST approximation of the internal rate of return of the investment project?

A   14.0%

B   17.6%

C   18.6%

D   20.0%

295 Which TWO of the following are relevant in capital investment decision-making using discounted cash flow methods of appraisal?

	Relevant?
Annual depreciation	
Cost of capital	
Sunk costs	
Timing of future cash flows	

296 A company has decided to lease a machine. Six annual payments of $8,000 will be made with the first payment on receipt of the machine. Below is an extract from an annuity table:

Year	Annuity factor
	10%
1	0.909
2	1.736
3	2.487
4	3.170
5	3.791
6	4.355

The present value of the lease payments at an interest rate of 10% is $_____ (round to the nearest $)

297 What is the value after three years, to the nearest $, of $100 invested now at a compound rate of interest of 6% per annum?

A $18

B $19

C $118

D $119

298 A capital investment project requires expenditure of $90,000 in Year 0, followed by cash inflows of $30,000 at the end of each of the four years of the project's life. The project will have a terminal value of $60,000.

The payback period of the investment project is _____ years (round to the nearest year)

299 The following chart shows the discounted values of two investment projects:

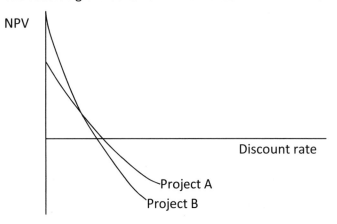

NPV

Discount rate

Project A
Project B

On the basis of the chart, which of the following statements are true?

	True
Project A has a higher internal rate of return than Project B	
Project A always has a negative NPV	
Project B has higher initial outlay than Project A	
Project B would be preferred if there is a zero cost of capital	

300 Discounted cash flow analysis is being applied to a project with the following results:

Rate of interest % per annum	Net present value $
13	9,362
19	(2,015)

Using the above results, what is the best approximation of the internal rate of return of the project?

A   13.8%

B   14.1%

C   17.9%

D   20.6%

Section 5

CASH MANAGEMENT

THE NATURE OF CASH AND CASH FLOW

301 **Working capital is most likely to increase when**

    A   work in progress falls

    B   selling prices increase

    C   credit period allowed to customers is reduced

    D   credit period taken from suppliers is increased

302 **Which of the following would not satisfy a definition of cash?**

    A   Current accounts and short-term deposits

    B   Bank overdrafts and short-term loans

    C   Foreign currency and deposits that can be quickly converted to your currency

    D   Long-term borrowing

303 **Which of the following is a capital payment?**

    A   Payment of salaries to directors

    B   Payment of interest on a loan

    C   Purchase of a motor vehicle

    D   Money raised from a new share issue

304 **Which of the following items would affect a company's cash flow but not its profits:**

    A   Payment of salaries to directors

    B   Payment of interest on a loan

    C   Depreciation of a motor vehicle

    D   Money raised from a new share issue

305 A business has received $9,000 in cash sales during the year. It has spent $5,000 in cash on expenses. It has receivables owing $1,000 at the year end and it owes suppliers $2,000 for goods and services received.

The net profit for the business on a cash accounting basis is $_____

306 **A company has provided the following information:**

Receivables collection period	38 days
Raw material inventory holding period	8 days
Production period (WIP)	4 days
Suppliers' payment period	28 days
Finished goods holding period	26 days

The working capital cycle for the business is _____ days.

307 **Which of the following businesses is most likely to have a negative working capital cycle?**

A   A supermarket

B   A firm of accountants

C   A construction company

D   A retailer offering 12 months interest free credit

308 **Which of the following is most likely to result in a cash inflow?**

A   Decrease in equity

B   Decrease in long term debt

C   Decrease in current assets

D   Decrease in current liabilities

CASH BUDGETS

309 A cash budget prepared for the forthcoming three months shows a substantial cash surplus in the first two months. Which TWO of the following would be suitable actions:

	True
Pay suppliers early to receive a cash discount	
Buy new plant and machinery	
Invest in treasury bills.	

310 Vincent is preparing a cash budget for July. His credit sales are as follows.

	$
April (actual)	40,000
May (actual)	30,000
June (actual)	20,000
July (estimated)	25,000

His recent debt collection experience has been as follows:

Current month's sales	20%
Prior month's sales	60%
Sales two months prior	10%
Cash discounts taken	5%
Irrecoverable debts	5%

Vincent can expect to collect $_____ from credit customers during July.

311 DRF's projected revenue for 20X9 is $28,000 per month. All sales are on credit. Receivables' accounts are settled 50% in the month of sale, 45% in the following month, and 5% are written off as irrecoverable debts after two months.

The budgeted cash collections for March are $_____

312 A company anticipates that 10,000 units of product z will be sold during January. Each unit of z requires 2 litres of raw material w. Actual inventories as of 1 January and budgeted inventories as of 31 January are as follows.

	1 January	31 January
Product z (units)	14,000	12,000
Raw material w (litres)	20,000	15,000

1 litre of w costs $4.

If the company pays for all purchases in the month of acquisition, what is the cash outlay for January purchases of w?

A $84,000

B $80,000

C $44,000

D $12,000

313 A company has a two-month receivables' cycle. It receives in cash 45% of the total gross sales value in the month of invoicing. Irrecoverable debts are 20% of total gross sales value and there is a 10% discount for settling accounts within 30 days.

What proportion of the first month's sales will be received as cash in the second month?

A   25%

B   30%

C   35%

D   55%

314 Spears makes gross sales of $40,000 per month, of which 10% are for cash, the rest on credit.

Experience shows the following:

Receivables paying

within one month	40%
within two months	50%
Settlement discounts (for payment within one month)	4%

Total expected cash receipts in any month will be

A $35,824

B $36,400

C $38,560

D $40,000

315 Selected figures from a firm's budget for next month are as follows.

Sales	$450,000
Gross profit on sales	30%
Decrease in trade payables over the month	$10,000
Increase in cost of inventory held over the month	$18,000

What is the budgeted payment to trade payables?

A $343,000

B $323,000

C $307,000

D $287,000

316 **A company has a current cash balance of $7,000, trade receivables of $15,000 and trade payables of $40,000. The company can sell goods costing $50,000 for £$70,000 next month.**

One half of all sales are collected in the month of sale and the remainder in the following month. All purchases are made on credit and paid during the following month. Inventory levels will remain constant during the month. General cash expenses will be $60,000 during the month.

The cash balance at the end of the month is overdrawn by $_____

317 Jasper has budgeted the following for a month:

	$000
Accounting profit after tax	100
Increase in receivables	35
Increase in inventory	20
Increase in trade payables	20
Depreciation	70
Increase in provisions	
Taxation	40

What is the budgeted increase in cash balances for the month?

A $55,000

B $125,000

C $175,000

D $225,000

318 A business has experienced the following sales figures (in $000) over the last three years:

Year	Jan to Apr	May to Aug	Sep to Dec
20X1	60	94	65
20X2	64	99	68
20X3	70	106	71

The business uses a three period moving average technique to determine both a trend line and seasonal variations.

What is the seasonal variation for September to December 20X2?

A   +$11,000

B   +$31,000

C   -$11,000

D   -$31,000

319 **Which of the following statements is true when there is a high level of inflation in an economy?**

A   Lenders will require a higher rate of return

B   The retail price index (RPI) will fall

C   The value of financial assets (such as debt) increases

D   A company's cost of capital will fall

320 Which of the following statements regarding cash budgets are false?

A   Cash budgets can help determine when future investments can be made

B   Cash budgets can help to plan for the arrangement for future short term financing

C   Cash budgets can be used as a control tool for an organisation

D   Cash budgets are created independently from other functional budgets

CASH MANAGEMENT

321 A company is considering increasing its credit period to customers from one month to two months. Annual revenue is currently $1,200,000. It is expected that the increased credit period would increase sales by 25% and result in an increase in profit of $45,000, before any INCREASE in finance charges have been taken into account. The company's cost of capital is 10%.

What is the financial effect of this proposal, after taking into account any increase in finances charges?

A   Increase in profit of $35,000

B   Decrease in profit of $35,000

C   Increase in profit of $30,000

D   Decrease in profit of $30,000

322 A UK local authority, which is governed by The Local Government Act 2003, want to make an investment of surplus funds in a non-approved investment.

The level of the proceeds from the investment that have to be set aside as provision for credit liabilities (PCL) is _____ %

323 A business policy is that one member of staff deals with cash receipts recording whilst another staff member reconciles cash receipts to sales and banking records.

This is an example of what?

A   Segregation of duties

B   Accountability

C   Physical cash security

D   Reconciliation

324 **Which TWO of the following are not normally roles that a treasury manager would undertake?**

	NOT a role of a treasury manager?
Raising finance	
Collecting debts	
Investing in short-term assets	
Credit control	

325 **Which of the following would be considered to be poor physical security measures with respect to the handling of cash?** *(select all that apply)*

	Poor security?
Safe combinations are the same for all safes	
Keys are kept in a locked cabinet	
Cash counting is not performed in a visible area	
Cash is only banked once a month	

INVESTING AND FINANCING

326 **For which of the following types of investment might the capital value vary?** *(select all that apply)*

	Variable capital value?
Equity shares held in a listed company	
Sterling Certificates of Deposits	
Unnegotiable local authority deposits	
Instant access deposits	

327 Which of the following investments is likely to provide the lowest level of return?

    A   Gilts

    B   Certificates of deposit

    C   Local authority stock

    D   Bank deposits

328 GYH plc has just taken out a loan that involves repaying mainly interest payments each period with only a small amount of principle repaid during the life of the loan. The bulk of the capital will be repaid on maturity.

    What type of repayment pattern is being described here?

    A   Bullet

    B   Balloon

    C   Mortgage-style (amortising)

    D   Irredeemable

329 6% Treasury stock is currently valued at $92 and is redeemable in one year's time. What is the redemption yield?

    A   6%

    B   6.5%

    C   8.7%

    D   15.2%

330 Which of the following is likely to have a fixed return per annum?

    A   Coupon yield

    B   Redemption yield

    C   Interest yield

    D   None of the above

331 Which of the following would not be considered to be an external influence on cash balances?

    A   Interest rates in the economy

    B   Company treasury management policies

    C   Economic recessions

    D   Changes in banks' willingness to lend

332 UNQ has an overdraft limit of $60,000. In March the company is $25,000 overdrawn. Overdraft interest is charged at 1% per month.

    The overdraft interest charged in March will be $_____

Section 6

PROVIDING INFORMATION

INFORMATION FOR COMPARISON

323 An adverse material usage variance could be caused by which TWO of the following?

	Cause of variance?
The storeroom supplying less material than is required by production	
The purchase of cheap material	
Poorly maintained machinery	
A series of short deliveries	

324 Which of the following situations is likely to cause an adverse material usage variance?

A   A world shortage of the material used

B   Employing unskilled machine operators

C   Machinery idle time

D   Limited storage space

325 The following is a report of the budgeted and actual costs for a production department during March.

	Master budget Units	Flexed budget Units	Actual Units
Sales (units)	10,000	9,000	9,000
	$	$	$
Direct materials cost	50,000	45,000	46,000
Direct labour cost	40,000	36,000	39,000
Fixed production overheads	70,000	70,000	69,000
Total costs	160,000	151,000	154,000

The total variable cost variance for the month was $_____ favourable

336 **A flexible budget is:**

A   a budget showing variable production costs only

B   a budget showing actual costs and revenues in the budget period

C   a budget which shows the costs and revenues at different levels of activity

D   a budget that is changed monthly

337 **What term describes: 'the forecasting of differences between actual and planned outcomes, and the implementation of action, before the event, to avoid such differences'?**

A   Feedforward control

B   Variance analysis

C   Budgeting

D   Feedback control

338 **A variance report comparing actual results achieved during a month with the budgeted performance for the month is an example of:**

A   control action

B   feedback control

C   feedforward control

D   reporting by exception

339 A business prepared the following budget for the year:

	$	$
Sales		640,000
Direct costs	250,000	
Overhead costs	330,000	
Total costs		580,000
		60,000

One-third of overhead costs are variable costs. Actual results for the year were to make and sell only 90% of the budgeted quantities. Sales revenue was $570,000 and costs were $565,000.

What was the sales price variance for the year?

Sales price variance

A $6,000 Adverse

B $6,000 Adverse

C $64,000 Adverse

D $70,000 Adverse

340 A product has a budgeted direct labour cost of $6 per unit. In a period, production volume was as follows:

Budget   8,000 units

Actual   7,700 units

Actual direct labour costs for the period were $47,600.

The total direct labour cost variance due to rate and efficiency factors was $_____

Place a tick to indicate whether the variance was favourable or adverse:

	Favourable	Adverse
Total direct labour cost variance		

341 **A product has a budgeted direct materials cost of $12 per unit. Production volume for the period was:**

Actual   6,750 units

Budget   6,500 units

Actual direct materials cost for the period were $79,840.

What was the total direct material cost variance?

The total direct material cost variance was $_____

Place a tick to indicate whether the variance was favourable or adverse:

	Favourable	Adverse
Total direct material cost variance		

342 A business prepared the following budget for the year:

	$	$
Sales		640,000
Direct costs	250,000	
Overhead costs	330,000	
Total costs		580,000
		60,000

One-third of overhead costs are variable costs. Actual results for the year were to make and sell only 90% of the budgeted quantities. Sales revenue was $570,000 and costs were $565,000.

What was the total cost variance (due to price and usage issues) for the year?

A $15,000 Adverse

B $21,000 Favourable

C $21,000 Adverse

D $15,000 Favourable

343 Which of the following factors should be the least likely to affect a decision about whether or not to investigate a variance reported during a particular month in the middle of the financial year?

    A   Size of the variance

    B   Whether it is favourable or adverse

    C   Whether it is likely to be controllable

    D   The trend in the monthly variance over the year to date

344 What is the principle of reporting by exception with variance analysis?

    A   Report variances only occasionally

    B   Report only those variances that exceed a certain limit

    C   Report only to the most senior management

    D   Report only adverse variances

345 A business makes and sells a product for which the budgeted sales were 200 units each month. At the end of month 7, actual sales for the year to date were 1,250 units. A revised forecast prepared at the end of month 7 indicated that actual sales for the year in total were likely to be 2,000 units.

Applying the concept of feedforward control, what sales volume variance should be reported at the end of month 7?

    A   150 units adverse

    B   250 units adverse

    C   400 units adverse

    D   550 units adverse

346 Which TWO of the following statements relating to the application of feedback and feedforward control are true?

	True
Feedback and feedforward are both applied in budgetary planning and control.	
Feedback is used in the analysis of variances.	
Feedforward enables budgeted data for a period to be amended for the next period.	
Feedforward relates to the setting of performance standards.	

347 Which one of the following is not a factor that should affect a decision as to whether to investigate a variance?

    A   Controllability of variance

    B   Cost of investigation

    C   Personnel involved

    D   Trend of variance

348 **Which one of the following is the correct description of a flexible budget?**

    A   A budget that can be changed according to circumstances

    B   A budget that is adjusted according to actual activity

    C   A budget that is open to negotiation

    D   A budget that is used for planning purposes only

349 A product has a budgeted direct material cost of $5 per unit. In a period, production of the product was:

Budget   9,000 units

Actual   8,800 units

$44,380 was incurred on direct materials for the period's production.

The total direct material cost variance due to price and usage factors was $_____

Place a tick to indicate whether the variance was favourable or adverse:

	Favourable	Adverse
Total direct material cost variance		

REPORTING MANAGEMENT INFORMATION

350 **What is an ad hoc report?**

    A   A report that contains standard information that is printed out regularly, often at set times.

    B   A report that contains non-standard information that is printed out regularly, often at set times.

    C   A report that may be generated only once or occasionally. It will not have a set content and the content will vary according to requirements.

    D   A report that may be generated only once or occasionally. It will have a set content, according to requirements.

351 Non-financial managers are likely to experience problems in understanding and interpreting management accounting reports.

Which of the following statements is the *least* appropriate method of dealing with this problem?

    A   Highlight and explain any unusual items in the report

    B   Discuss with users the most appropriate form of report

    C   Include clear graphics and charts, and ensure that the narrative is as simple as possible

    D   Ensure that only individuals with some accounting knowledge are appointed to management positions

352 Written communication is usually used when:

    A   a permanent record is required

    B   only one person needs to be given some information

    C   someone wants to know something simple very quickly

    D   someone wants to know something simple that requires no consideration

353 A company manufactures three products and wants to show how sales of each product have changed from 20X1 to 20X8. Which of the following charts or diagrams would be most suitable for showing this information?

    A   Pie chart

    B   Component bar chart

    C   Simple bar chart

    D   Multiple bar chart

354 XYZ produces three main products. Which would be the most appropriate chart or diagram for showing total turnover and its product analysis month by month?

    A   Area chart

    B   Line graph

    C   Pie chart

    D   Component bar chart

355 Confirmation, acknowledgement, covering and circular are all types of:

    A   letter

    B   memo

    C   data

    D   information

356 You work in the accounts department of a company. Your friend in the sales department has requested some accounting information and assures you that the finance director is aware of this request. You should:

    A   Print out the information and give it to them

    B   Give them your computer password and let them use your computer

    C   Decline the request

    D   Confirm the request with the finance director

357 Which of the following is not an advantage of component bar charts

    A   The relative importance of each component can be assessed

    B   The information can be interpreted quickly

    C   More than one component can be displayed at a time

    D   The total value can be easily assessed and determined

358 The following spreadsheet shows an extract from a company's sales figures.

	A	B	C	D	E
1	Sales				
2					
3			2010	2011	2012
4	Region				
5	NW		10,000	12,000	11,500
6	NE		7,000	6,200	8,200
7	SE		3,000	10,000	12,000
8	SW		1,500	5,750	5,600

The management accountant wishes to produce a chart to demonstrate the trends over time between the different regions.

Which of the charts would be suitable? *(select all that apply)*

	Suitable?
Stacked (compound) bar chart	
Line charts	
Pie charts	

359 **What would be the most effective way of demonstrating a trend in new mobile telephone sales from January to December 20X1?**

A   Pie chart

B   Bar chart

C   Table

D   Line graph

360 **Which of the following graphs would best be used to identify trends in data**

A   A bar chart

B   A pie chart

C   A line graph

D   A scatter graph

361 **Which of the following graphs would best be used to illustrate that two variables are uncorrelated**

A   A bar chart

B   A pie chart

C   A line graph

D   A scatter graph

Section 7

ANSWERS

SECTION 1: MANAGEMENT INFORMATION

MANAGEMENT INFORMATION

1

	Correct?
Cost accounting can be used for inventory valuation to meet the requirements of internal reporting only	
Management accounting provides appropriate information for decision making, planning, control and performance evaluation	✓
Routine information can be used for both short-term and long-run decisions	✓
Financial accounting information can be used for internal reporting purposes	✓
Management accounting information must be presented in a prescribed industry format	

Cost accounting can be used for inventory valuation to meet the requirements of both internal reporting and external financial reporting. Management accounting is not regulated and organisations will often present it in a different way to even other organisations within the same industry. The other statements are correct.

2   A

An exception report is not prepared regularly. Instead it tends to be produced when something exceptional or out-of-the-ordinary has occurred.

3   C

Revenue is most likely to be based on the quantity delivered and the distance travelled. In addition, costs are likely to relate to both distance travelled and weight of load. Cost per tonne/km gives a measure of both quantity and distance.

4   C

A and B are elements of product cost and D is factory overheads which are all included in the cost accounts.

5   A

Investment centre managers are responsible for capital investment decisions as well as costs, sales revenues and profits of their division. Their performance is generally measured by return on capital measures such as ROCE and residual income.

6   D

	$
Opening WIP	3,000
Direct materials	12,500
Direct labour	21,500
Production overhead absorbed	17,400
	54,400
Transfer to finished goods	(49,000)
Therefore closing WIP	5,400

7

	WIP control	Finished goods control	Stores ledger control	Production overhead control
Debit	✓			
Credit			✓	

Direct materials are taken out of stores (therefore credit Stores account) and put into production (so debit WIP account).

8

	WIP control	Finished goods control	Stores ledger control	Production overhead control
Debit	✓			
Credit				✓

Absorbed production overhead costs are added to production costs, so debit WIP account. The corresponding double entry is to credit the Production overhead control account.

9

	WIP control	Finished goods control	Cost of sales account	Production overhead control
Debit		✓		
Credit	✓			

Completed production leaves WIP (therefore credit WIP account) and is put into finished goods inventory (so debit finished goods control account).

10   D

The financial accounts should include only items that will be included within the financial statements published by the company. They should not include notional rent or notional interest. In contrast, since the cost accounts are used to prepare information for management, they can include notional cost items such as notional rent. For example, a cost centre might be charged notional rent for its occupation of a building owned by the organisation, in order to make its costs fairer in comparison with another cost centre that occupies rented premises.

11   C

Indirect materials are a charge to production overheads. When indirect materials are issued from inventory, we debit the Production overhead account (adding to the expenditure) and credit the Materials/stores account (reducing the asset balance).

12   C

When production overhead is over absorbed, the credit entry in the Production overhead account for overheads absorbed is higher than the debit entries in the same account for overhead expenditure incurred. The over-absorbed overhead is therefore accounted for by:

- debiting Production overhead account;

- crediting Over-absorbed overhead account.

13   B

Useful management information should be clear to the user and relevant for purpose. It will not be provided whatever the cost as the cost of providing the information should not exceed the benefit. The level of detail and degree of accuracy will depend on the use to which the information will be put. Timeliness may override the need for complete accuracy and senior management may require less detail than operational management.

14

	Features of graphical users interfaces
Icons	✓
Keyboard	
Optical mark reading	
Pull-down menu	✓

Icons and pull down menus are features of the software graphical user interfaces. Keyboards and optical mark reading are examples of hardware devices.

15   C

Marginal costing is used mainly for decision making and is not a feature of financial accounting.

16   C

Item B describes the costs of an activity or cost centre. Item A describes cost units. Item D describes budget centres. A cost centre is defined as 'a production or service location, function, activity or item of equipment for which costs can be ascertained'.

17   C

Managers are responsible for planning, control and decision making and require information for these purposes. Research and development is a function in an organisation.

18   D

An interlocking bookkeeping system has separate cost and financial ledgers; the financial ledger contains asset and liability accounts. Control accounts are a feature of all bookkeeping systems. An integrated system has one set of ledger accounts.

19   B

	Used to capture and store data
Bar code	✓
Disk	✓
Printer	
Tape	✓

Bar codes are used for the capture of management accounting data. Disks and tape are used for storage. A printer is an output device.

20   D

Direct costs are debited to the Work-in-progress account and labour costs will be credited from Wages control.

21   C

The report will help managers to decide whether an investment is worthwhile.

22   D

Useful management information does not necessarily have to be presented in report format, supported by calculations or communicated in writing.

23   D

Option A is describing an integrated system. Option B does not describe a system for bookkeeping and all systems are supported by prime entry records. Option D is the description of an interlocking bookkeeping system.

24   D

Options B and C could be cost centres, profit centres or investment centres. Option A describes an investment centre.

25   A

Options B and C are senior management activities. Option D is the responsibility of the stores manager.

26   A

Management accounting information is not used by external stakeholders and it consists of information for planning and decision making as well as control so (ii) and (iii) are incorrect.

27   D

28

	True
In an integrated accounting system there will be a cost ledger control account	
An integrated accounting system has one combined set of ledger accounts	✓
An interlocking accounting system has separate cost and financial ledger accounts	✓

COST CLASSIFICATION AND COST BEHAVIOUR

29   C

Prime cost is defined as the total direct production cost of an item. This consists of direct material and direct labour cost, plus any direct expenses.

30   C

This is a simple definition of a semi-variable (semi-fixed) cost.

31   D

Material costs vary with the volume of production.

32   B

An overhead cost is an indirect cost. This is a cost that cannot be traced directly to a unit of production or sale, or any other cost unit. Overheads include indirect materials costs, indirect labour costs and indirect expenses (for example, factory rental costs, machinery insurance costs, machinery depreciation and so on).

33

	Correct definition
A cost which cannot be influenced by its budget holder	
Expenditure which can be economically identified with a specific cost unit	✓
Cost which needs to be apportioned to a cost centre	
The highest proportion of the total cost of a product	

A direct cost is a cost that can be traced directly to a unit of production or sale, or another cost unit. 'Economically' means that the benefit from identifying and tracing the direct cost to the cost unit must be worth the cost and the effort. In practice, this means that low-cost items, particularly low-cost material items, might be treated as indirect costs because the benefit from the greater 'accuracy' from treating them as direct material costs is not worth the cost and the effort.

34   D

All four items could be treated as direct materials costs. However, staples are a very low-cost material item, and it would probably not be worth the effort to treat them as direct material costs to gain greater accuracy in costing. Instead, the cost of staple purchases will probably be treated as an overhead expense. (This illustrates the point that a direct cost is expenditure that can be identified with a specific cost unit, but only if it is 'economical' to do so.)

35   C

A would be a line parallel with the base line showing units. B would be a line commencing at '0'. D would show a stepped effect, fixed for a short range, with successive increases.

36   Using the high-low method, the estimate of the overhead cost if 16,200 square metres are to be cleaned is $88,095

	$
Total cost of 15,100 square metres	83,585
Total cost of 12,750 square metres	73,950
	_____
Variable cost of 2,350 square metres	9,635
	_____

Variable cost is $9,635/2,350 square metres = $4.10 per square metre.

Fixed costs can be found by substitution:

	$
Total cost of 12,750 square metres	73,950
Variable cost of 12,750 square metres (× $4.10)	52,275
	_____
Fixed costs	21,675
	_____

So for 16,200 square metres:

Overheads   = $21,675 + (16,200 × $4.10)   = $88,095

37   C

	$
Total cost of 18,500 hours	251,750
Total cost of 17,000 hours	246,500
	_____
Variable cost of 1,500 hours	5,250
	_____

Variable cost per hour = $5,250/1,500 hours = $3.50.

	$
Total cost of 17,000 hours	246,500
Less variable cost of 17,000 hours (× $3.50)	59,500
	_____
Balance = fixed costs	187,000
	_____

38   B

Period	Output	$
2	35,480	55,893
1	29,720	48,981
Difference	5,760	6,912

Variable cost per unit $\dfrac{\$6,912}{5,760}$ = $1.20 per unit

For period 1	Total cost	$48,981
	Variable cost (29,720 × $1.20)	$35,664
	Fixed cost	$13,317

39   C

The fixed cost per unit doubles. If you are not sure about this, you can try a simple numerical example. Suppose that a production process has fixed costs of $1,000 per month. If it produces 1,000 units in the month, the fixed cost per unit will be $1. If output falls 50% to 500 units per month, the fixed cost per unit will go up to $2 – i.e. there will be an increase of 100% in the fixed cost per unit.

40   B

A, C and D are all variable costs and would be best described as a linear graph.

41   C

Conversion costs are the costs of converting raw materials into a finished manufactured product. They consist of direct labour costs, direct production expenses (if any) and production overhead costs.

42   The estimated variable production costs per unit if the high-low method is **$10.65**

Using the high-low method

		$
High output	14,870	254,554
Low output	12,610	230,485
Difference	2,260	24,069

Therefore variable cost per unit = 24,069/2,260 = $10.65

43   B

A semi-variable cost is a cost which has a fixed element and a variable element. If activity increases, the variable element will remain constant per unit. The fixed element will reduce as a cost per unit. For example, if there are fixed costs of $100 and output is 100, fixed cost per unit will be $1. If output increases by 10%, fixed cost per unit will be $0.909. This is a percentage reduction of 9.1%.

The overall percentage reduction in the cost per unit will depend on the proportion of variable to fixed costs but it is unlikely to be in proportion to the change in activity.

44   C

Profit = $60/3

Selling price = Total cost + Profit = $60 + $20 = $80

45   C

Variable cost = $(10 + 29 + 3 + 7 + 2) = $51. The total variable cost includes non-manufacturing variable costs.

46   C

Prime cost = $(10 + 29 + 3) = $42. Prime costs are direct costs, and exclude all overheads.

47   C

[($218,200 – $207,000) ÷ (110,000 – 100,000 units)]

48   C

Answer A would appear as a curve. Answer B would cause an increase in the cost per unit. Answer D is irrelevant as far as the standard costs per unit are concerned, since this would not affect the overheads.

49   B

Job costing is used for work carried out at the specific request of a customer. Process, service and batch costing all use averaging to arrive at the final cost per unit.

50   B

Fixed costs	= Total costs – Total variable cost
	= $156,980 – (7,400 × $12.20)
	= $66,700

51   C

Total cost per unit at 6,000 units = ($60,000 + $42,000)/6,000 = $17

Total cost per unit at 8,000 units = ($76,000 + $50,000)/8,000 = $15.75

The reduction in cost per unit = $17 – $15.75 = $1.25

52   D

Option A represents direct materials and should be coded between 1000 and 1999. Option B represents a production overhead and should be coded between 4000 and 4999. Option C represents a production overhead. Although it is 'materials' it is not materials directly included in product production. It should be coded between 4000 and 4999. Option D is the correct answer.

53   B

54   A

	Apply to straight line depreciation
Indirect	✓
Period	✓
Production	
Variable	

55   A

[($8,000 ÷ 1,000 units) – ($8,000 ÷ 1,250 units)]

56   B

	Only appear in cost accounts
Cash discounts available to customers	
Interest charged to products based on average inventory	✓
Notional rent for the use, by different cost centres, of company-owned buildings	✓
Trade discounts received from suppliers	

57   C

58

	Cost units
Cost per length of cloth	
Cost of the design department	✓
Cost of the stitching team	✓
Cost per dress	
Cost of material handling	✓

A cost centre is where costs are traced or grouped, typically due to an activity. It is typically a unit, team or department within an organisation such as the stitching team, the design department or the material handling team. The other options in the scenario are cost units and are not cost centres.

SECTION 2: COST RECORDING

ACCOUNTING FOR MATERIALS

59   B

Using FIFO, inventory is issued at the earliest price.

The issue on the 19 January would be made up of 500 costing		$1,250
	1,000 costing	$2,750
	600 × $2.80	$1,680
The issue on the 31 January would be made up of 1,000 × $2.80		$2,800
	800 × 2.90	$2,320
		─────
Total issue value		$10,800

60   C

Using LIFO, the 1,900 units of closing inventory is valued as the opening inventory of 500 units ($1,250) plus the 1,000 units received on 4 January ($2,750) plus 400 of the units received on 11 January, which have a value of $4,480 × 400/1,600 = $1,120.

	$
400 units of opening inventory	1,250
1,000 units received on 4 January	2,750
400 units received on 11 January	1,120
	─────
Total value of closing inventory	5,120
	─────

61   D

With cumulative weighted average cost method, a new average cost only needs to be calculated before there is an issue from stores.

	Units	Total cost	Average cost
		$	$
Opening inventory	500	1,250	
Receipts on 4 January	1,000	2,750	
Receipts on 11 January	1,600	4,480	
Receipts on 18 January	1,200	3,480	
	─────	─────	
	4,300	11,960	$2.78
Issues on 19 January	(2,100)	(5,838)	$2.78
	─────	─────	
	2,200	6,122	
Receipts on 25 January	1,500	4,350	
	─────	─────	
	3,700	10,472	**$2.83**
Issues on 31 January	(1,800)	(5,094)	**$2.83**
	─────	─────	
	1,900	5,378	
	─────	─────	

62   The number of units of materials that must be put into the process is **632** units.

$$\text{Input} = \text{Output} \times \frac{100\%}{(100\% - \text{wastage rate percentage})}$$

So if the required output is 600 units, the input material requirements are:

$$\text{Input} = 600\,\text{units} \times \frac{100}{(100 - 5)}$$

= 631.57 units, or 632 units to the nearest whole unit.

63   The valuation of closing inventory if LIFO is used is **$460**

	Units	Unit cost	Total
		$	$
Opening inventory	100	3.00	300
3 March receipt	200	3.50	700
	300		1,000
8 March issue	(250)	200 at 3.50	(700)
		50 at 3.00	(150)
	50	3.00	150
15 March receipt	300	3.20	960
17 March receipt	200	3.30	660
Balance prior to issue	550		1,770
21 March issue	(500)	200 at 3.30	(660)
		300 at 3.20	(960)
	50	3.00	150
23 March receipt	450	3.10	1,395
	500		1,545
27 March issue	(350)	3.10	(1,085)
Closing balance	150		460

The closing inventory balance represents 50 units at $3 and 100 units at $3.10.

64 The valuation of issues using the weighted average method of inventory valuation at each issue is **$3,548**

	Units	Unit cost	Total
		$	$
Opening inventory	100	3.00	300
3 March receipt	200	3.50	700
	300	3.333	1,000
8 March issue	(250)	3.333	(833)
	50	3.333	167
15 March receipt	300	3.20	960
17 March receipt	200	3.30	660
	550	3.249	1,787
21 March issue	(500)	3.249	(1,625)
	50	3.249	162
23 March receipt	450	3.10	1,395
	500	3.114	1,557
27 March issue	(350)	3.114	(1,090)
Closing balance	150	3.114	467

Issues = $833 + $1,625 + $1,090 = $3,5483

65 **A**

The actual wastage was 480 kg, which represents 4% of the 12,000 kg input into the process. The expected loss was 3% and the difference between the actual and expected loss is 1%.

66

	Poor procedures
Ordering in bulk in order to reduce order costs	✓
Having one staff member responsible for ordering and checking deliveries	✓
Demanding material requisition notes from production departments	
Performing regular inventory volume checks	
Using goods received notes to update inventory records	

67 **D**

A and C are relevant only to physical inventory movement. B is a description of the LIFO method.

68   A

B and D are incorrect as material costs which are lower, reduce cost. C is incorrect as lower costs lead to higher profit.

69   B

To avoid the risk of a stockout, the re-order level should be set at a level to provide for a maximum delivery time and a maximum usage during the delivery time. Here, this is:

2 months × 2,000 units per month = 4,000 units

70   B

A material requisition note is a document used internally for requisitioning a quantity of inventory from the stores.

71   D

$$\text{EOQ} = \sqrt{\frac{2C_oD}{C_h}} = \sqrt{\frac{2 \times (50+5) \times 4,000}{(15 \times 0.1)+0.2}}$$

$$= \quad 509 \text{ units}$$

72   In the formula $Q = \sqrt{2C_oD/C_h}$, if Co = \$20, D = 24,000 and Q = 400, then Ch is **\$6.00**

$$400 = \sqrt{\frac{2 \times \$20 \times 24,000}{C_h}}$$

Square both sides of the equation:

(400 × 400)	=	(2 × \$20 × 24,000)/C_h
160,000	=	\$960,000/C_h
160,000C_h	=	\$960,000
C_h	=	\$6

73   D

A: production volume should not cause differences in inventory.

B: damage or waste should be recorded on the individual inventory records.

C: such a request should be entered on the inventory record.

74   A

$$\text{EOQ} = \sqrt{\frac{2 \times 10 \times 15,000}{0.10 \times 12}} = 500 \text{ units}$$

When using the EOQ formula, use annual demand and annual holding cost (or monthly demand and monthly holding cost).

75

	Used in calculating the EOQ
The cost of storing materials	✓
The cost of interest incurred in financing materials	✓
The purchase of inventory	
The cost of ordering materials	✓
The cost of insuring materials	✓

Costs 1, 2 and 4 are examples of holding costs. Purchase costs are not included in the EOQ as they are assumed not to change regardless of the size of the order.

76   D

FIFO would charge production with earliest costs. Using the weighted average method (whether periodic or cumulative) would result in a mix of earliest and latest costs.

77   A

If inventory is returned to stores but this is not recorded, physical inventory will be higher than the record reflects; in addition, the production to which the inventory was originally charged will still be carrying the cost and thus will have a higher value than it should have.

78

	True	False
Production costs will be lower using weighted average pricing rather than LIFO.	✓	
Profit will be higher using LIFO pricing rather than FIFO.		✓
Inventory values will be lower using FIFO pricing rather than weighted average.		✓

When prices are rising, closing inventory values will be higher with FIFO than weighted average cost, and higher with weighted average cost than with LIFO. Statement 3 is incorrect.

When prices are rising, the cost of sales is higher with LIFO, followed by weighted average cost, followed by FIFO. When the cost of sales is higher, profit is lower. Statement 1 is therefore correct and statement 2 is incorrect.

79   A

It is assumed that inventory is consumed at a constant rate through the year.

Average inventory (250 units ÷ 2)   125 units
Annual stockholding cost/unit $3
Total annual stockholding cost $375

80   B

The economic order quantity is calculated as the square root of [(2 × Cost of placing an order × Annual demand), divided by the annual holding cost for one unit of the item of inventory]. Items A, C and D are therefore most relevant to the EOQ calculation. Purchase price is sometimes used to help calculate a stockholding cost but it is not otherwise required.

81   The maximum inventory control level would be calculated as **7,800** units

	Units
Re-order level	6,000
Usage during the delivery period (1 month × 1,800 units)	(2,700)
Re-order quantity	4,500
Maximum inventory control level	7,800

82   C

Inventory will fluctuate between 3,200 kg, on receipt of an order, and 1,200 kg (the minimum inventory held).

The average stockholding is therefore $\dfrac{3,200 + 1,200}{2}$ = 2,200 × \$1.20 = \$2,640

83

	Matched with the good received note
Invoice from supplier	✓
Purchase order	✓
Purchase requisition	
Stores requisition	

An invoice is matched to a goods received note and a purchase order before payment is made.

84   The value of the issue on Day 7 is **\$376.25**

The total cost for the period is = \$500 + \$375 + \$200 = \$1,075

The average cost for the period is \$1,075/200 units = \$5.375 per unit.

Multiplied by the issue on Day 7 of 70 units the issue is valued at \$376.25 (70 units × \$5.375 per unit).

85   C

Maximum inventory control level = Re-order quantity + Re-order level – (Minimum demand × Minimum lead time)

= 1,400 + 1,600 – (600 × 1)

= 2,400 kg

86 C

Minimum inventory control level = Re-order level – (Average demand × Average lead time)

= 1,600 – (1.5 × 700)

= 550 kg

87 D

Authorisation should be obtained, if the stores function is to be properly maintained. Answer A ignores stores issues and returns. A stores requisition must detail other information, such as quantities required. The lead time is the time from ordering to delivery from the supplier.

88 A

The introduction of buffer inventory would increase average stockholding. So (iii) is correct. Total holding cost would increase but holding costs per unit should stay the same or may even decrease so (i) is incorrect. The Economic Order Quantity is dependent on the cost of ordering per order, annual demand and unit holding costs, none of which should change so EOQ should not be affected. Total ordering cost should not be affected.

89 C

The EOQ model minimises ordering (purchasing) and stockholding cost for a given annual demand. The re-order level depends on the average lead time and usage of material and is set so that stockouts are unlikely to occur. It does not depend on the EOQ.

90

	True	False
Inventory values will be higher using last-in first-out (LIFO) rather than weighted average.		✓
Profit will be lower using weighted average rather than first-in first-out (FIFO).	✓	

When prices are rising consistently, issues using FIFO will be at a lower cost than issues using LIFO, and profit is higher, because they will be the earliest (lowest price) materials received. Closing inventory using FIFO will therefore be higher as the earlier (lowest priced) materials will have been issued out. Weighted average prices and inventory values always fall between LIFO and FIFO values. Statement 1 is incorrect and Statement 2 is correct.

91

	Raw materials returns
Goods received note	
Materials returned note	✓
Materials requisition note	
Delivery note	

A materials returned note is used to record materials sent back to stores from production. A materials requisition note is a request from production to stores for material. A goods received note is produced by the stores department to record the receipt of goods into stores and a delivery note is provided by the supplier when goods are delivered.

92

	$5,252	$5,330	Debit	Credit
Material inventory		✓		✓
Work-in-progress		✓	✓	

The cost per unit of the material received on 7 May is $6,500/500 = $13 per kg. LIFO values issues at the latest price so the material issued on that date is valued at 410 × $13 = $5,330. The accounting entry for an issue of material to production is to debit WIP and credit material inventory.

93   **A**

The re-order level is set assuming usage and lead time will be at the maximum as these are the conditions for which the quantity of material required will be at the highest. Setting the re-order level at this level should mean that stock-outs are avoided.

94   **B**

Using the formula and rearranging to find c:

$$\sqrt{\frac{2 \times c \times 12,000}{1.50}} = 800$$

$24,000c = 1.50 \times 800^2$

$c = 960,000/24,000 = 40$

95   **B**

96   **B**

$[(860 \times 2.2) + (50 \times 2.25)]$

97

	Used in calculating the maximum inventory control level
Maximum lead time	
Minimum usage	✓
Reorder level	✓
Reorder quantity	✓

ACCOUNTING FOR LABOUR

98 The direct wages for January would be **$32,000**

Unless overtime is worked specifically at the request of a particular customer, the cost of any overtime premium is treated as a general production overhead cost. The only direct labour cost is the cost of the hours worked, valued at the basic rate of pay per hour. Here, this cost is $27,500 + $4,500 = $32,000.

99 C

	Hours
750 units should take (at 20 units per hour)	37.5
Did take	32.0
Time saved	5.5

100 B

	$
600 units at $0.40	240.0
50 units at $0.50	25.0
10 units at $0.75	7.5
For 660 units	272.5

101 H&H employed on average 55 employees during the year. There had been 8 leavers all of whom were replaced. The company's labour turnover ratio was **14.55 %**

Labour turnover ratio = 8/55 × 100% = 14.55%

102 B

Working conditions, pension provisions and welfare are all costs associated with *retaining* labour, not *replacing* labour.

103 B

Piecework is an incentive-based pay scheme, because employees are paid more for producing more, and so have an incentive to be more productive. A high day rate scheme, in which employees receive a high basic rate of pay, does not offer an incentive to be more productive.

104 D

Efficiency compares the standard hours produced with the hours actively worked

(9,300 hours ÷ 9,200 hours) × 100% = 101%.

105 A job is budgeted to require 3,300 productive hours after incurring 25% idle time. If the total labour cost budgeted for the job is $36,300, the labour cost per hour is **$8.25**

Productive hours	3,300
Idle time (3,300 × 25/(100 – 25))	1,100
Total paid hours	4,400
Total labour cost	$36,300
Labour rate per hour	$8.25

106 B

Managers are not usually classified as direct labour.

107 D

A: idle time is partially controllable. B: not all internal factors are controllable. C may not be production staff's responsibility.

108 B

Idle time is an overhead cost. Unless overtime is worked specifically at the request of a particular customer, the cost of any overtime premium is treated as a general production overhead cost. However, when overtime is worked specifically for a customer, the overtime premium is treated as a direct cost of the job.

	$
42 hours less 4 hours idle time = 38 hours	
38 hours at basic rate of pay ($6.60)	250.80
Overtime premium for 2 hours (× 50% of $6.60)	6.60
Total direct wages cost	257.40

109 C

The efficiency ratio is given by:

$$= \frac{\text{Actual output in standard hours}}{\text{Actual hours}} \times 100\% = \frac{380/0.5 \times 100\%}{780\,\text{hours}} = 97.44\%$$

110 C

Capacity ratio × Efficiency ratio = Activity ratio

Capacity ratio = 103.5/90 × 100% = 115%

111 B

1,065 units should take	2,556 minutes
did take	2,250 minutes (37.5 × 60)
	————
Saving	306 minutes or 306/60 = 5.1 hours

Total earnings		
Basic wages	37.5 × $8.50	318.75
Bonus	5.1 × $8.5/3	14.45
		————
		$333.20

112 C

A incorrectly calculated as $15/day guarantee. B incorrectly based entirely on piecework earnings. D incorrectly calculated as piecework earnings + day rate guarantee.

113 B

Premiums arising as a result of overtime worked at a customer's request will be charged as a direct cost of that job; the premium on overtime due to general operating conditions will, however, be treated as an indirect cost. Labour pay relating to direct work on production (basic pay or piecework payments) will also be charged as a direct cost.

114 The amount charged to production overhead would be **$2,650**

Production operatives' overtime is treated as an overhead cost. Therefore:

	$
20 × 6 × $2.50	300
10 × 44 × $5	2,200
10 × 6 × $2.50	150
	————
	2,650
	————

115 The total amount paid if output is 620 units is **$317**

(500 × 0.5) + (100 × 0.55) + (20 × 0.6) = $317

116

	Used to allocate costs
Overtime hours of direct operatives at basic rate	✓
Overtime premiums of factory employees	
Productive time of direct operatives	✓
Training of direct operatives	

Overtime premiums and training are normally treated as overhead costs.

117

	Used to allocate costs
Employee record card	
Attendance record card	
Timesheet	✓
Job card	✓

A timesheet and a job card are used to allocate labour costs to cost units. An attendance record card is used for payroll purposes and an employee record card details all of the information relating to an employee.

118 D

119 D

120 A

121 A

The capacity ratio measures the number of hours available compared to budget. A ratio that is greater than 100% means that more actual hours were worked than budget.

122 C

$[(10 - 8) \times 0.5 \times 8]$

123 D

$(2{,}350 \div 2{,}320) \times 100$

124

	Used in the financial accounting system
Wages and salaries control account	✓
Wages and salaries payable account	✓
Wages and salaries overtime account	
Wages and salaries overhead account	

125 B

The bonus and overtime premium payments would be classified as indirect labour cost. The only direct labour cost will be the total hours at the standard rate per hour.

= 50 hours × $10.50 per hour = $525.00

ACCOUNTING FOR OTHER EXPENSES

126 An invoice for the Whitby site for power would be coded as **100/420/620**

100 for Whitby followed by 420 for power followed by 620 for production. Power costs are most likely to be a production overhead cost, rather than a purchasing, finance or sales overhead cost.

127

	Production overhead costs
Wood used as raw material	
Rubber covers for handles	
Depreciation	✓
Power	✓
Sales manager's salary	
Labour in assembly department	
Oils and greases	✓
Telephone and postage	
Insurance of plant	✓
Supervisory labour	✓

Wood used as raw material and rubber covers for handles are direct material costs. Sales manager's salary is a selling overhead cost. Labour in assembly department is a direct labour cost. Telephone and postage is likely to be treated as an administration overhead.

128 A

Expected useful life in machine hours = 5 years × 3,000 hours per year = 15,000 hours

Depreciation rate = $45,000/15,000 = $3 per machine hour

Depreciation charge for the period = 810 hours × $3 = $2,430

129 D

Factory insurance costs are overhead costs. Administrative salaries are a non-production cost. Assembly labour used in production is a direct labour cost. Costs incurred hiring a special machine for a specific job are a direct expense of that job

130 C

No matter which method of depreciation is used, the aim should be to charge the same total amount of depreciation over the life of the asset. With straight-line depreciation, the depreciation charge is the same each year. With the reducing balance method, the charge is higher in the earlier years and reduces over each succeeding year. Answer C is correct.

131

	Production overhead costs
Training of direct operatives	✓
Wages of distribution staff	
Normal idle time in the factory	✓
Productive time of direct operatives	
Sales personnel salaries	

Wages of distribution staff and sales personnel salaries are not production costs. Productive time of direct operatives is a direct labour cost.

132 B

The reducing balance method of depreciation results in higher depreciation charges in the earlier years compared to the straight-line method although depreciation in total will be the same. A, C and D are therefore incorrect.

133

	True	False
Using the reducing balance method, product unit costs decline from year to year if output stays the same.	✓	
Using the straight-line method, product unit costs decline as output increases.	✓	

Using the reducing balance method, depreciation charges are higher in the earlier years and lower in the later years, so if output stays the same Statement 1 is correct.

Using the straight-line method, depreciation charges are the same each year. If output increases the cost per unit will fall so Statement 2 is correct.

134 A

Capital expenditure is the cost of buying or adding to non-current assets. Manufacture of goods is revenue expenditure. Stationery expenditure is normally treated as revenue expenditure, and machinery bought for resale would be classed as inventory and deemed to be revenue expenditure.

SECTION 3: COSTING TECHNIQUES

ABSORPTION COSTING

135 C

This is not a sound rationale for determining the absorption cost of a product (the organisation may not even use marginal costsing).

136 A

137 A

Using pre-determined overhead absorption rates will often lead to under- or over-absorption of overheads if actual overheads differ from the budgeted overheads. The other options are all benefits derived from using pre-determined overhead absorption rates.

138 A

	Acceptable method?
Direct labour hours	✓
Machine hours	✓
As a % of prime cost	✓
$x per unit	✓

Production overheads can be absorbed by any of the methods listed in the question. A rate per unit is only appropriate when all units produced are identical.

139 The amount re-apportioned to the Finishing cost centre would be **$31,577**

Total requisitions = (6,000 + 6,500 + 3,200 + 1,200) = 16,900

Re-apportionment rate per requisition = $82,100/16,900 = $4.858

Re-apportioned to Finishing cost centre = 6,500 requisitions × $4.858 = $31,577

140 D

Absorption costing is a method of calculating a cost per cost unit that includes direct costs and a share of overhead costs. A fully absorbed cost is therefore the sum of direct costs and overheads. Overhead costs can be a mix of variable and fixed overheads. D is therefore the only possible answer to this question.

141 D

Over or under absorption can only be determined with actual activity and actual overheads, together with machine hour rate.

142 C

	Machine hours	Labour hours
Cutting department	✓	
Finishing department		✓

Cutting is machine intensive and finishing is labour intensive so it is more accurate to base overhead absorption rates on machine hours and labour hours respectively.

143 B

Absorption is the attribution of costs to cost units; apportionment is the splitting of shared costs between cost centres; re-apportionment is the splitting of service cost centres' costs between production cost centres.

144

	$450	$1,450	Under	Over
Absorption of overheads	✓			✓

Over/(under) absorption = Absorbed overheads – Incurred overheads

Since variable overhead costs were as budgeted ($5 per unit), there was no under or over absorption of variable overheads.

Budgeted fixed overhead = 3,000 units × $9 = $27,000

Actual production volume = 3,500 units – 300 units = 3,200 units

	$
Fixed overhead absorbed (3,200 × $9)	28,800
Fixed overhead incurred ($27,000 × 1.05)	28,350
Over-absorbed fixed overheads	450

145 B

Machine hour rate = $180,000/10,000 machine hours = $18 per machine hour

Machine hours are more appropriate than labour hours as a basis for recovering/absorbing overhead costs, because the enterprise has a machine-intensive operation, with more machine hours of operation than direct labour hours worked. A unit basis for absorbing overhead is inappropriate because the enterprise makes a wide range of different products.

146 B

	$
Overhead absorbed	71,890
Overhead incurred	73,220
Under absorbed overhead	1,330 (under absorbed because absorbed < actual)

147 The total overheads included in production department 1 will be **$27,871**

Using the repeated distribution method

	P1	P2	S	M
Allocated and apportioned	17,500	32,750	6,300	8,450
Apportion M	6,338	1,690	422	(8,450)
			6,722	–
Apportion S	4,033	2,689	(6,722)	
Final allocation and apportionment	27,871	37,129		

148 The actual machine hours were **91,000 hours.**

Pre-determined absorption rate = $180,000/90,000 = $2 per hour

Over absorption = ($4,000)

($4,000) = Absorbed overheads (Actual machine hours × $2) – Actual overheads ($178,000)

Absorbed overheads (Actual machine hours × $2) = $178,000 + $4,000

Absorbed overheads (Actual machine hours × $2) = $182,000

Actual machine hours = $182,000/$2 = 91,000

149 D

Any method that approximates to the relative usage of the resource by departments is acceptable; all three methods given are reasonable.

150

	Over-absorbed	Under-absorbed	Impossible to determine
Machining department			✓
Assembly department			✓

To calculate the amount of overhead over absorbed or under absorbed, we need to calculate the amount of overhead that has been absorbed. This information is not available from the figures provided. The figures are for budgeted expenditure and actual expenditure, but not for overheads absorbed.

151 D

Personnel services are likely to relate to all staff, not just direct operatives; therefore D would be the most appropriate.

152

	$1,200	$1,540	Under	Over
Absorption of overheads		✓	✓	

	$
Overhead absorbed	125,200
Overhead incurred	126,740
	————
Under absorbed overhead	1,540
	————

As less overhead is absorbed than the actual overhead incurred, overheads were under absorbed.

153 B

Overhead absorbed	2,180 × $12	$26,160
Overhead incurred		$25,470
		————
Over-absorbed overhead		$690

154 The overhead absorption rate per machine hour is **$ 13.35**

Machine hours = 216,000/120   = 1,800 hours

Overhead absorption rate   = Overhead cost/machine hours

                               = $24,030/1,800 = $13.35 per machine hour

155 The total re-apportionment to Production Cost Centre Y is **$51,120**

	X	Y	A	B
Total overhead cost			42,000	57,600
Re-apportion A	16,800	25,200	(42,000)	
Re-apportion B	31,680	25,920		(57,600)
		————		
		51,120		

156 A

Overhead absorption rate = $164,000/10,000 = $16.40 per direct labour hour

	$
Overhead absorbed (9,800 × $16.40)	160,720
Actual overhead	158,000
	————
Over absorbed overhead	2,720

157 A

Under or over absorption is determined by comparing what was actually spent with what has been absorbed using the standard overhead absorption rate.

158 A

To determine over/under absorption, the level of actual fixed overhead cost and the fixed overhead absorbed would need to be known. Statement 1 is not possible to determine.

To determine profit, sales revenue and cost would need to be known for both periods. Statement 2 is not possible to determine.

159 The absorption cost per unit will be **$ 124**

Fixed overheads per unit = $800,000 / 40,000 units = $20

Marginal cost per unit = $104

Absorption cost per unit = $104 + $20 = $124

160 The fixed overhead cost of a Bomber is **$20.00**

Cutting department:

Budgeted hours = (6,000 × 0.05) + (6,000 × 0.10) = 900 hours

Absorption rate for the cutting department = $120,000/900 = $133.33

Stitching department:

Budgeted hours = (6,000 × 0.20) + (6,000 × 0.25) = 2,700 hours

Absorption rate for the stitching department = $72,000/2,700 = $26.67

Fixed overhead cost of a Bomber = (0.10 × $133.33) + (0.25 × $26.67) = $20

161 If actual overheads were $694,075, the budgeted overhead absorption rate per hour was $20.50 per hour

	$
Actual fixed overhead	694,075
Under-recovered overhead	35,000
	———
Absorbed fixed overhead	659,075
	———

Actual consulting hours: 32,150

Absorption rate = $659,075/32,150 hours = $20.50 per hour

162 D

	A	B	C	D
Overhead expenditure ($)	18,757	29,025	46,340	42,293
Direct labour hours	3,080	6,750		
Machine hours			3,380	2,640
OAR ($ per hour)	6.09	4.30	13.71	16.02

Thus D is the highest rate per hour.

163 D

164 A

165 C

Number of units produced = 56,000 + 4,000 = 60,000

OAR = $258,000/60,000 = $4.30 per unit

Total production cost per unit = $3.60 + $4.30 = $7.90

	$
Sales revenue	700,000
Cost of sales (56,000 × $7.90)	442,400
Gross profit	257,600
Less non-production cost	144,000
Net profit	113,600

166 C

$520,800 + {(122,000 × 0.45) + [(96,600 + 24,400) × 0.7]}

167 The budgeted overhead absorption rate per client hour was **$9.00 per hour**

[(21,720 − 345) ÷ 2,375]

168

	Included in product costs?
Direct overhead costs	
Fixed overhead costs	✓
Variable overhead costs	✓

169 The gross profit for the period was **$38,350**

{169,000 − [(93,130 + 41,540) × 6,500/6,700]} = $38,350

170 D

171 The absorption cost per unit **$23**

Fixed overhead cost per labour hour = $60,000 / 15,000 = $4 per hour

Fixed overhead cost per unit = $4 per hour × 2 labour hours = $8

Absorption cost per unit = $15 (marginal cost) + $8 = $23

172

	Result from the use of predetermined rates?
Delay in the establishment of job costs	
Change in unit costs reflecting seasonal activity	
Overhead over or under recovery	✓

(ii) is not affected by overhead absorption. If predetermined overhead absorption rates are used there will be no delay in establishing job costs as the rate is calculated at the beginning of the year and can be used as required. So (i) is incorrect. It is likely that there will be over or under recovery of overheads as, at any time, overhead costs and/or estimated activity may differ from the budgeted figures used to set the overhead absorption rate. (iii) is correct.

MARGINAL COSTING

173 C

Inventory is valued at marginal production cost, which is the prime cost plus any variable production overhead.

174 Using a marginal costing system the actual profit for December would be **$61,400.**

Flexed budget profit = (Actual production × Budget contribution per unit) − Budgeted fixed costs

Budget contribution per unit = ($150 − $110) = $40

Budgeted fixed costs = 2,500 × $15 = $37,500

$54,500 = (Actual production × $40) − $37,500

Actual production = ($54,500 + $37,500)/$40 = 2,300 units

Actual materials cost = $5 × 1.2 = $6 per litre

Actual variable overheads cost = $6 × 0.7 = $4.2

Actual contribution = ($150 − $50 − (6 × $6) − (5 × $4.2)) = $43

Actual profit = (2,300 × $43) − $37,500 = $61,400

175 B

Under absorption costing, inventory is valued at full production cost

= $16.30 + $11.60 = $27.90

The change in the level of inventory in the period is given by the difference between sales and production

Units produced	33,300
Unit sold	(33,950)
	———
Decrease in stock	(650)
Valued at $27.90	$18,135

176 The fixed production overhead cost per unit was **$5.**

$10,000/2,000 = $5/unit.

177 B

Fixed costs are not considered when calculating contribution.

178 The profit made under an absorption costing system was **$47,000**

	$	$
Sales (9,000 × $20 per unit)		180,000
Production cost of sales (9,000 × $(2 + 3 + 3 + 4))		108,000
		———
		72,000
Production overhead absorbed (11,000 × $4)	44,000	
Production overhead incurred (10,000 × $4)	40,000	
	———	
Over-absorbed overhead		4,000
		———
		76,000
Variable selling costs (9,000 × $1)		9,000
Fixed selling costs (10,000 × $2)		20,000
		———
Profit		47,000
		———

179 The profit using a marginal costing system was **$39,000**

$47,000 – (2,000 × $4) = $39,000

Alternatively:

	$
Sales (9,000 × $20 per unit)	180,000
Variable cost of sales (9,000 × $(2 + 3 + 3 + 1))	81,000
	———
Total contribution	99,000
Fixed production costs (10,000 × $4)	40,000
Fixed selling costs (10,000 × $2)	20,000
	———
Profit	39,000
	———

180

	Higher	Lower
Profit		✓
Inventory value		✓

In marginal costing fixed costs are charged against profits in the period that they are incurred and they are not included in inventory. Both profit and inventory would be lower using marginal costing.

181 B

Machine operators' wages, royalty fees and raw materials are all variable costs of production. Factory rent is a fixed production overhead and would not be charged to inventory under marginal costing.

182 A

Profit differs if there is a movement of inventory in the period. In this case there is an increase of 1,000 units (97,000 – 96,000). When inventory increases in a period the marginal costing profit is less than the absorption costing profit by the amount of fixed overhead included in inventory i.e. $1,400, since this overhead is carried forward under absorption costing but charged as a period cost in full under marginal costing.

183

	True	False
Inventory value at the end of the period would be higher than at the beginning of the period.	✓	
Inventory values both at the beginning and at the end of the period would be higher using absorption rather than marginal costing.	✓	

Inventory has increased by (84,000 – 82,000) 2,000 units in the period. Statement 1 is true.

Inventory values are always higher using absorption rather than marginal costing because a proportion of fixed overhead is included in the valuation of the product units. Statement 2 is true.

184

	True
In a marginal costing profit statement, variable selling costs are deducted before contribution is calculated	✓
In an absorption costing profit statement, all fixed costs are shown together	
Absorption costing treats total fixed costs as period costs	
Examining contribution per unit is a better way to determine the impact on profit of a change in sales volume than examining profit per unit	✓

185 The increase in profit will be **$20,000**

Existing contribution = $40 per unit × 6,000 units = $240,000

Revised contribution = $(70 – 18) × 5,000 units = $260,000

Increase in profits = $260,000 – $240,000 = $20,000.

186 C

Absorption costing is a costing system in which inventory valuation includes a share of all production costs, whereas using marginal costing fixed production costs are not allocated to product units. D is clearly incorrect as inventory values cannot include non-production costs. Answer A is also a correct statement as, with absorption costing product costs include both prime cost and production overhead. It does not completely and accurately explain the distinction between absorption and marginal costing, however, as marginal costing may include the variable elements of prime cost and production overhead in the product cost.

187 A

Closing inventory has increased by (10,000 – 9,760) 240 units in the period. Profit will be higher if absorption costing is used because a proportion of fixed production overhead will be carried forward into a future period to match against sales.

188 C

Inventory values are always lower using marginal costing as they do not include a share of fixed production overhead cost. Inventory levels have fallen so profit will be higher using marginal costing as a share of fixed production overhead from a previous period will be charged against profit using absorption costing (relating to units produced in a previous period but sold in this period).

189

	$10,000	**$11,200**	**$11,500**	**$12,000**
Absorption costing profit				✓
Marginal costing profit	✓			

190

	True	**False**
Inventory value will always be lower than when using absorption costing	✓	
Profit will always be higher than when using absorption costing	✓	

191 C

[(50 – 26.1) × 1,100] – 21,600

192 B

The gross profit margin is profit before selling and administration costs as a percentage of sales revenue. Option A is the net profit margin.

{$22/unit – 11.6 – (($7,200 + 16,400) ÷ 4,000 units)} × 100 ÷ 22 = 20.5%

193 B

Inventory has increased during the period so absorption costing profit will be higher than marginal costing profit by the amount of fixed overhead absorbed into each unit.

(200 units × ($7.5 – 4.8)/unit) = $540 higher

JOB AND BATCH COSTING

194 D

A bakery produces bread and cakes in batches. A brewery and a food canning business are likely to operate process costing systems.

195 D

Kitchen fitting consists of short jobs for customers, with each job being different. A shipbuilder will operate a contract costing system, and an oil refinery and a steel producer are likely to have process costing systems.

196 The sales price of Job 731 to the customer would have been **$24,860**

To answer this correctly, you need to identify that when the profit margin is 25% of the sales price, this means that it is one-third of the cost. (Selling price = 100%, profit = 25%, so cost = 75% of sale. Therefore profit is 25/75 = 1/3 of cost.)

	$
Direct materials	4,250
Direct labour (1,000 hours)	7,200
Production overhead (1,000 hours × $5.50)	5,500
Production cost	16,950
Administrative overhead (10%)	1,695
Total cost	18,645
Profit (1/3 of cost)	6,215
Sales price	24,860

197 D

Job costing is used to calculate the cost of individual orders for customers, where each order or 'job' is different in some way, and jobs cannot be treated as standard items of output.

198 D

The tools are a direct cost of the job.

199 C

Unit costing is relevant in a production environment where large numbers of identical units are produced. Service costing relates to a business which provides a similar service to many customers, measured in units such as passenger-miles (transport) or bed-days (hospital). Batch costing is relevant to a production situation where batches of relatively small numbers of identical units are produced; production may then switch to a batch of a different product.

200 The selling price of Job XX is **$6,228**

$3,633/0.7 = $5,190

Note that a gross profit margin means a margin on gross profit (i.e. before the deduction of expenses). If the question had stated net profit margin or just profit margin the answer would have been $6,228.

201 C

	$
Sales price	1,690
Profit (× 30/130)	390
	———
Total cost	1,300
Overhead	694
	———
Prime cost	606
	———

202 C

	Part of job costs?
Actual direct material cost	✓
Actual direct labour cost	✓
Actual manufacturing overheads	
Absorbed manufacturing overheads	✓

A typical job cost includes actual material and labour cost and absorbed overhead.

203 B

{[460 + (600 × 2.2)] ÷ 0.8}

204 D

Idle time is 10% of total hours so productive hours represent 90% of the total.

((630 ÷ 0.9 hours) × $12/hour) = $8,400

205

	Overheads?
Salaries of supervisors, each of whom are responsible for two cost centres, where no record is kept of their time in each cost centre	
Wages of skilled operators assigned to individual jobs, in particular cost centres, with time recorded on time sheets	
Wages of labourers who are moved from cost centre to cost centre and who maintain detailed time sheets. They are not assigned to work on specific orders in each cost centre.	✓

206 A

207

	True	False
Cost control in job costing is less important than in traditional costing		✓
Cost control in batch costing is less important than in traditional costing		✓

Cost control is equally important in both job costing and batch costing as it is in traditional costing. The systems employed may differ slightly, but the goals will still be the same.

208

	Strong cost control
Timesheets are completed and examined at the end of the job	
The client is charged a mark-up on actual job costs	
Materials requisitions are approved by a job supervisor	✓
Regular checkpoints are implemented for examining cost-to-date	✓

Time sheets should be completed and examined regularly. For jobs which are likely to be long in duration (such as in this example on the construction industry) it is unlikely to be appropriate to only examine time sheets at the end of the job).

If a client is charged a mark-up on ACTUAL costs then there will be no incentive to control costs at all. If costs rise the client will simply be charged a higher fee. There would be a stronger incentive to control costs if the client is charged a fee based on budgeted costs (which will mean that the client's fee is set in advance and that the construction company must bear the cost of any costs which are out of control).

The other options are good cost controls.

PROCESS COSTING

209 D

Normal loss = 5% of 10,000 tonnes = 500 tonnes

In process costing, normal loss is valued at its scrap value in the process account. 500 tonnes × $2 = $1,000.

210 The number of tonnes accounted for as abnormal losses or abnormal gains in the month were **50 tonnes**

	Tonnes
Input	10,000
Normal loss (5%)	500
Expected output	9,500
Actual output	9,450
Therefore abnormal loss	50

211 A

Expected output = 30,000 – 3,000 = 27,000 units

Total costs = $180,000 + $25,000 + $145,000 = $350,000

Total costs less scrap value of normal loss = $350,000 – (3,000 × $3) = $341,000

Cost per unit = $341,000/27,000 = $12.63

212 D

Abnormal losses will only be valued at nil if they have no scrap value.

213 The valuation of the output was **$22,040**

Normal loss = 10% of 3,000 units = 300 units. Value of normal loss (at $1.50 per unit) = $450

$$\text{Cost/unit} = \frac{\$(9,000+11,970-450)}{3,000 \quad 300} = \frac{\$20,520}{2,700} = \$7.60$$

Valuation of output = $7.60 × 2,900 = $22,040

214 D

	Output (kg)	Sales value ($)	Apportionment of joint costs ($)	
Product A	2,000	24,000	(24/96)	7,500
Product B	4,000	72,000	(72/96)	22,500
		96,000		30,000

215 C

Normal loss = 25% of 3,500 units = 875 units. Value of normal loss (at $8 per unit) = $7,000.

Process account

	Units	$		Units	$
Materials	3,500	52,000	Normal loss	875	7,000
Labour		9,625	Output	2,800	???
Abnormal gain	175	???			
	3,675			3,675	

$$\text{Cost/unit} = \frac{\$(52,500+9,625-7,000)}{3,500 \quad 875} = \frac{\$55,125}{2,625} = \$21$$

Valuation of output = $21 × 2,800 = $58,800

216 A

Abnormal losses are unexpected and must be valued at the total cost of a normal unit.

217

	Used to apportion joint costs?
Weight	✓
Sales revenue	✓
Selling prices	
Net realisable value	✓

1, 2 and 4 are all recognised ways of splitting joint costs. Selling prices (i.e. per unit) are not an acceptable basis as this does not take into account the relative volumes of each joint product.

218 C

$$\text{Cost per unit} = \frac{\text{Input cost} - \text{Proceeds from normal loss}}{\text{Input units} - \text{Normal loss units}}$$

$$= \frac{\$7,000 - (50 \times \$10)}{500 - 50} = \$14.44$$

219 A

This is the reverse situation to that of having scrap proceeds form normal loss, so instead of crediting proceeds to the process account, costs will be debited to the process account (adding to the costs to be attributed to other units).

220 The amount of material input to production in the period was **7,738 kgs**

Let I = the amount of material input into the process.

The normal loss is 20% × I = 0.2I

Therefore the expected output is 80% × I = 0.8I

There is an abnormal gain of 4% of I = 0.04I

The expected output + the abnormal gain = the actual output

So   0.8I + 0.04I = 6,500

        0.84I = 6,500

    I = 6,500/0.84 = 7,738

Alternative approach

An abnormal gain means that actual losses were less than the expected loss. The actual loss was 20 − 4 = 16%. Therefore the actual input = 6,500/100 − 16% = 6,500/0.84 = 7,738.

221 D

Abnormal losses and abnormal gains are always valued at the same cost as good output which is:

$$\frac{\text{Total production cost}}{\text{Normal output}}$$

Abnormal gains are a debit entry in the process account.

222

	True	False
The higher the net realisable value of normal losses the lower will be the cost per unit of normal output.	✓	
The higher the abnormal losses the higher will be the cost per unit of normal output.		✓

Cost per unit of normal output is:

$$\frac{\text{Cost of process} - \text{Net realisable value of normal loss}}{\text{Expected output}}$$

Therefore statement 1 is true.

Abnormal losses do not affect the cost per unit of normal output so statement 2 is false.

223 D

Total loss is 10%. If output is 4,000, input must be 4,000 ÷ 0.9 = 4,444.

224 C

This will avoid poor decisions on individual products based on joint costs which cannot be avoided for an individual product.

225 C

Total sales revenue	= ($18 × 10,000) + ($25 × 20,000) + ($20 × 20,000)
	= $1,080,000
Joint costs to be allocated	= $277,000 – ($2 × 3,500) = $270,000
Allocation rate = (270,000/1,080,000)	= 0.25 of sales revenue.
Joint costs allocated to Product 3	= 0.25 × (20 × 20,000)
	= $100,000
	= ($100,000/20,000 units) = $5 per unit

226 A

	Kg
Input	12,000
Normal loss	1,200
Expected output	10,800
Actual output	10,920
Abnormal gain	120

227

	True	False
In costing for joint products, apportioning joint costs using net realisable values will always result in higher costs being apportioned to each product than using volume of output.		✓
The benefit of further processing should be evaluated on the basis of incremental costs and revenues only.	✓	

The method of apportionment does not affect the total overhead cost apportioned to products, just the share given to each product. The benefits of further processing should be evaluated on the basis of incremental costs and revenues.

228 C

In process costing the cost per unit is calculated by dividing the net cost of the process (total costs less the scrap value of normal loss) by the expected output from the process (total units less normal loss). {($216,720 − (1,200 units × $2/unit)) ÷ (24,000 − 1,200 units)} = $9.40

229

	True	False
Using the sales value method of cost apportionment, and where there is no further processing, the gross profit margin of each product will be the same.	✓	
Using the units of output method of cost apportionment, the joint cost per unit will be the same for all joint products.	✓	

230 B

SERVICE COSTING

231 D

Items A, B and C are costs associated with hospitals, transport companies and hotels respectively.

232 C

	$
Vehicle cost	16,000
20X3 depreciation	(4,000)
	———
	12,000
20X4 depreciation	(3,000)
	———
	9,000
	———
20X5 depreciation	2,250

	$
Drivers' wages	13,500
Fuel	8,500
Maintenance	750
Tax and insurance	1,000
Depreciation	2,250
	26,000

233 D

234 D

	Not applicable to service costing
Allocating costs between fixed and variable elements	
Unique nature of the work	✓
Accurate time recording	
Work that extends beyond one accounting period	✓
Accuracy in valuing work in progress	

235 D

236 The cost per tonne/kilometre in the week was **$2.15**

Journey	Load (tonnes)	Distance (kms)	Tonne/kms
1	5	80	400
2	7	100	700
3	3	40	120
4	5	60	300
5	4	150	600
		Total	2,120

Total cost per tonne/km = $4,558/2,120 = $2.15

237 The cost per customer was **$6.70.**

There are 15 tables available with 4 seats each for 9 hours a day for 30 days in the month, so at 100% occupancy there would be 16,200 customers (as each stay an hour). There is only 60% occupancy, so cost per customer can be calculated by dividing the total cost by 16,200 × 0.6.

($65,124 ÷ (30 × 9 × 15 × 4 × 0.6 customers)) = $6.70

SECTION 4: DECISION-MAKING

COST/VOLUME/PROFIT ANALYSIS

238 D

Sales price per unit = $45,000/5,000 = $9

Variable costs per unit = $7

Contribution per unit = $2

Fixed production costs = $29,000 – (5,000 × 5) = $4,000

Fixed administration costs = $12,000 – (5000 × 2) = $2,000

Therefore breakeven point (Fixed overhead/contribution per unit) =

$6,000/2 = 3,000 units

This represents a 2,000 unit drop from existing sales which is 40% margin of safety (2,000/5,000).

Option 1 is wrong as it ignores variable selling costs when calculating contribution

Option 2 is wrong as it uses administration costs as the fixed overhead figure

Option 3 is wrong as it puts the numerator and denominator the wrong way round

239 D

Original contribution per unit = $15 – $6 = $9

Original break-even point = $43,875/$9 = 4,875 units

New contribution per unit = $20 – $5 = $15

New fixed costs = $43,875 × 120% = $52,650

New break-even point = $52,650/$15 per unit = 3,510 units

The new break-even point is 1,365 units lower than the original break-even point.

240 C

$$\text{Break-even number of units} = \frac{\text{Fixed costs}}{\text{Contribution per unit}}$$

If the selling price per unit and the variable cost per unit both rise by 10%, then the contribution per unit also rises by 10%. Given no change in fixed costs, the break-even number of units will therefore decrease.

(This assumes that the product earns a positive contribution in the first place!)

241 C

Budgeted fixed costs = 1,000 × ($5.80 + $4.60) = $10,400

Contribution per unit = $(24.90 – 5.60 – 3.40) = $15.90

Break-even point = $10,400/$15.90 per unit = 654 units

242 In a period when actual sales were $140,000, AL's margin of safety, in units, was **2,000**

Break-even point in sales revenue = Fixed costs/Contribution to sales ratio

= $48,000/40% = $120,000

If actual sales = $140,000, then the margin of safety is $20,000 ($140,000 − $120,000) in terms of sales revenue.

Since the selling price is $10 per unit, this is equivalent to 2,000 units.

243 C

Contribution per unit = $(65 − 22 − 14 − 9) = $20.

	$
Budgeted fixed costs (12,000 × $10)	120,000
Required profit	18,000
Required contribution	138,000

Volume of sales required to achieve target contribution and profit = $138,000/$20 per unit = 6,900 units

244 The break-even point (to the nearest whole unit) is **3,125 units**

Contribution per unit = $26 − $10 = $16

Break-even point = $50,000/$16 per unit = 3,125 units

245 The profit at an activity level of 1,000 units would be **$16,250**

	$
Direct materials	2,500
Direct labour	5,000
Variable production overhead (50% × 1,000)	500
Variable selling costs (80% × 1,250)	1,000
Total variable costs for 500 units	9,000
Sales revenue for 500 units	17,500
Total contribution for 500 units	8,500
Total contribution for 1,000 units (8,500 × 2)	17,000
Fixed production overhead (50% × 1,000)	(500)
Fixed selling costs (20% × 1,250)	(250)
Profit for 1,000 units of sale	16,250

246 A

Break-even = 80% of 5,000 units = 4,000 units

Total contribution at 4,000 units = (4,000 × $25) = $100,000

Profit at 4,000 units = $0

Fixed costs are therefore $100,000

247 B

The definition of a margin of safety is actual or budgeted sales compared with sales required to break even.

248 C

	Before	After
Sales price	100	110
Variable cost	60	60
Contribution	40	50

The increase in contribution from 40 to 50 is an increase of 25%.

249 The break-even sales revenue is **$300,000**

Total fixed cost = $137,500 + $27,500 = $165,000

Contribution/sales ratio = 275/500 = 55%

Break-even sales revenue = Fixed costs/C/S ratio

= $165,000/55% = $300,000

250 C

	$
Fixed costs	210,000
Target profit	65,000
Target contribution	275,000

	$
Sales	640,000
Variable costs	384,000
Contribution	256,000

Contribution/sales ratio = 256,000/640,000 = 40%

Sales revenue required to achieve target profit = $275,000/40% = $687,500

251 C

Sales price per unit = $640,000/128,000 = $5

	$
Fixed costs	210,000
Target profit	52,000
Target contribution	262,000

Contribution/sales ratio = 40% (see previous solution).

Sales revenue required to achieve target profit = $262,000/40% = $655,000

Sales units required to achieve target profit = $655,000/$5 = 131,000 units

252 B

$$\text{Break-even point} = \frac{\text{Fixed cost}}{\text{Contribution per unit}}$$

$$\text{So, } 24,600 = \frac{\$(77,000 + 46,000)}{\text{Contribution per unit}}$$

Contribution per unit = $123,000/24,600 = $5

253 A

254 C

Contribution = $100,800 – $60,480 = $40,320

C/S ratio = 40,320/100,800 = 0.4

$$\text{Sales revenue required} = \frac{\$(36,000 + 5,000)}{0.4} = \$102,500$$

255 The margin of safety (sales units) is **12,000 units**

Contribution per unit = $40,320/112,000 = $0.36

Break-even point = $36,000/0.36 = 100,000 units

Margin of safety is 112,000 – 100,000 = 12,000 units

256 C

$$\text{Target value} = \frac{\text{Target contribution}}{\text{Unit contribution}} = \frac{\text{Target profit} + \text{Fixed costs}}{\text{Unit contribution}}$$

$$= \frac{\$(250,000 + 1,600,000)}{\$(130 - 50)} = 23,125 \text{ units}$$

257   The contribution/sales ratio is **48.6%**

Contribution = Sales price – Variable cost = $(17.50 – 7.60 – 1.40) = $8.50

C/S ratio = 8.5/17.5 × 100% = 48.6%

258   The sales revenue (to the nearest $000) is required to break even is **$854,000**

Break-even sales revenue = Fixed costs/C/S ratio

Contribution = $(1,000,000 – 590,000) = $410,000

C/S ratio = $410,000/$1,000,000 = 0.41

BEP = $350,000 ÷ 0.41 = $854,000

259   The net benefit to the company from further processing Product Y is **$20,000**

	$
Increase in income from further processing $(13 – 4) × 10,000	90,000
Increase in costs from further processing $7 × 10,000	70,000
	———
Net benefit from further processing	20,000
	———

SHORT-TERM DECISION-MAKING

260   In order to maximise profits, the product that Worth would prefer to produce first is product **E**

Materials requirements for maximum demand

=   (1.5 × 3,000) + (1 × 2,000) + (1.25 × 1,500) + (2 × 2,500)

=   13,375 kg of direct materials

There is enough material to meet maximum demand, so materials are not a limiting factor.

Labour requirements for maximum demand

=   (1 × 3,000) + (1 × 2,000) + (1.5 × 1,500) + (1.5 × 2,500)

=   11,000 hours

Labour is a limiting factor, since there are only 10,250 hours available.

Product	L	E	W	S
Contribution per unit	$10	$15	$12	$20
Labour hours per unit	1	1	1.5	1.5
Contribution per labour hour	$10	$15	$8	$13.33
Ranking	3rd-	1st	4th	2nd

261

	1st	**2nd**	**3rd**
X			✓
Y	✓		
Z		✓	

	X	*Y*	*Z*
Contribution per unit	$10	$9	$6
Minutes per unit	45	36	25
Contribution per minute	$0.222	$0.25	$0.24
Ranking	3rd	1st	2nd

262 C

Current costs *may* be relevant but only if they are indicative of future costs. Estimated future costs are only relevant if they are cash flows and are expected to occur as a direct consequence of the decision being taken.

263 The incremental effect of reworking and selling the material would be a loss of **$2,500**

The original cost is irrelevant. The material could be sold now for scrap for $12,500. If reworked, it could be sold for a net $10,000. The incremental effect of reworking is therefore a loss of $2,500.

264 D

Since Material R is in regular use and is readily available in the market, its relevant cost is the replacement price of $6 per kg.

The relevant cost of 1,000 kg = 1,000 × $6 per kg = $6,000.

265

	Not relevant?
Future costs	
Committed costs	✓
Sunk costs	✓
Incremental variable costs	
Incremental fixed costs	

Sunk (or historic) costs have already been spent and cannot be recovered. Committed costs cannot be changed by the decision and are not therefore considered relevant to the decision. All other costs in the list would normally be considered to be relevant to the decision.

266 B

Sunk costs include costs already incurred and committed costs are costs that will be incurred whatever happens. Answer A is therefore not a complete definition of sunk costs, and answer B is correct.

267

	Relevant?
Avoidable cost	✓
Future cost	✓
Opportunity cost	✓
Differential cost	✓

A future cost is a relevant cost provided that it is a cash flow arising as a direct consequence of the decision under consideration.

268 B

Relevant cost of:	$
250 skilled labour hours	
Basic pay (× $10)	2,500
Opportunity cost, contribution forgone (× $12)	3,000
750 semi-skilled hours	0
	_____
	5,500
	_____

269 The relevant labour cost of the contract is **$115,000.**

The manager who would be used as supervisor will be paid his full salary whatever the decision, so the manager's salary is not a relevant cost.

Cost of hiring skilled employees = 4 × $40,000 = $160,000

Cost of using internal staff = Replacement cost + Training cost = $100,000 + $15,000 = $115,000

Therefore retrain existing employees.

270 B

Materials are a limiting factor (workings not shown).

	Product I	Product II	Product III
Contribution per kg	$4.375	$5	$8
Ranking	3rd	2nd	1st

	Quantity	Materials needed
	Units	Kg
Product I (special contract)	1,000	8,000
Product III	2,000	12,000
		_____
		20,000
Product II (balance)	3,000	15,000
		_____
		35,000
		_____

271 A

	X	Y
Buy-in cost	$50	$80
Variable production cost	$42	$75
Extra cost to buy in	$8	$5
Hours per unit	0.40	0.50
Extra cost per hour	$20	$10
Ranking	1st	2nd

Product X should be prioritised for production (it is more expensive to buy in X than Y). Product X will use up all of the available labour meaning that all of Product Y must be bought-in and none of it can be produced in-house.

272 D

If you start up in business on your own, you will have to forgo your current salary with the insurance company.

273 D

This is the definition of an opportunity cost.

274 C

As the material is used regularly it will need to be replaced. Hence the replacement cost is the relevant cost.

275

Product	Rank
A	4
B	2
C	3
D	1

	Product A	Product B	Product C	Product D
Contribution per unit	$2.80	$2.60	$1.90	$2.40
Skilled labour hours*	1.4	1.2	0.9	1.0
Contribution/skilled labour hour	$2.00	$2.17	$2.11	$2.40
Priority	4th	2nd	3rd	1st

(*skilled labour hours = limiting factor)

276 B

Relevant costs	$
Skilled workers:	
Basic pay (100 × $9)	900
Opportunity cost of lost contribution (100 × $3.50 per hour)	350
Semi-skilled workers:	
Basic pay (200 × $5)	1,000
Management cost (zero, as it is fixed)	0
	———
Total relevant cost of labour	2,250
	———

277 The relevant cost of materials is **$2,000**

The historical cost of N is irrelevant. The relevant cost of N is its replacement cost, because if units of N are used, they will be replaced.

Relevant costs	$
N: 100 kg × $4 (replacement cost)	400
T: Lost scrap proceeds: 200 kg × $4	800
T: New inventory of T to be purchased: 100 kg × $8	800
	———
Total relevant cost of materials	2,000
	———

278 C

Contribution per $ of labour

A $\frac{6}{4}$ = $1.50/$

B $\frac{8}{4}$ = $2.00/$

(All other combinations either indifferent or A preferred.)

279 The best component to BUY-IN in order to maximise profit is Component **B.**

	A	B	C	D
Variable manufacturing cost ($)	6.00	8.00	9.00	11.50
Bought-in price ($)	11.00	11.50	13.00	16.00
Difference	5.00	3.50	4.00	4.50

Component B has the minimum extra cost of buying in. Note that, as all components use the same amount of labour, it is unnecessary to calculate the contribution per unit of limiting factor.

PRINCIPLES OF DISCOUNTED CASH FLOW

280 C

Cumulative discount factor at 8%, years 1 – 4 = 3.312

Cumulative discount factor at 8%, years 0 – 4 = 1.000 + 3.312 = 4.312

PV of $1,000 per annum, years 0 – 4 = $1,000 × 4.312 = $4,312

281 C

Let the annuity be $A

Cumulative discount factor at 5% for years 1 – 5 = 4.329

Present value = Annuity × Cumulative discount factor

$60,000 = 4.329 × A

$$\frac{\$60,000}{4.329} = A$$

A = $13,860

282 The present value of the lease at a discount rate of 12% per annum is **$50,624.**

Cumulative discount factor at 12% for years 0 to 9 = 1.000 + 5.328 = 6.328

(The discount factor is the annuity factor at 12% for years 1 to 9 plus a factor of 1.000 for the year 0 annuity).

Present value   = 6.328 × $8,000

                                  = $50,624

Allowing for rounding errors in the discount factor, the answer is clearly A.

283 C

Present value = Annuity × Cumulative discount factor

$33,550 = $5,000 × Cumulative discount factor, years 1 to 10

Cumulative discount factor = 6.710

From discount (annuity) tables, it can be found that the discount rate r that gives a cumulative discount factor of 6.710 for years 1 to 10 is 8%.

284 A

$$\text{IRR} \quad = 15\% + \frac{3,664}{(3,664 + 21,451)} \times (20\% - 15\%)$$

$$= 15.7\%$$

285 B

286 B

This is the definition of the IRR.

287 The present value of the interest on the loan is **$120,000.**

$$PV \quad = \frac{\$60k \times 10\%}{5\%}$$

$$= \$120,000$$

288 C

Year	Discounted cash flow at 10%	Cumulative discounted cash flow
0	(90)	(90)
1	27.3	(62.7)
2	24.8	(37.9)
3	22.5	(15.4)
4	20.5	5.1

Payback is between years 3 and 4.

289 B

The net present value is positive at 10% ($64,600 – $60,000) and negative at 15% ($58,200 – $60,000). Therefore the IRR must be between these two discount rates.

290 The investment at the start of the project is **$61,016.**

($18,000 × 3.791) – $7,222 = $61,016

291

	True
The discounted payback period at 10% will be longer than the discounted payback period at 20%.	
The discounted payback period at 20% will be longer than the discounted payback period at 10%.	✓
The non-discounted payback period will be longer than the discounted payback period.	
The non-discounted payback period will be shorter than the discounted payback period.	✓

The higher the cost of capital the lower the present values of future cash flows, therefore the longer the payback period. Statement 2 is correct.

Non-discounted cash flows will be higher than discounted cash flows so the payback period will be shorter. Statement 4 is correct.

292 The effective annual rate of interest of 2.1% compounded every three months is **8.67%.**

Using the formula $[(1.021)^4 - 1] \times 100 = 8.67\%$

293 B

Future incremental cash flows are an initial outflow of $100,000 followed by equal cash inflows of $30,000 each year. Therefore, assuming cash flows occur evenly through the year, the payback period is $100,000 ÷ $30,000 = 3.3 years.

294 A

Using the formula IRR   = 14% + [16,000/(16,000 + 10,500) × (20 − 14)%]

                = 14% + (0.604 × 6%)

                = 14% + 3.624% = 17.6%

295

	Relevant?
Annual depreciation	
Cost of capital	✓
Sunk costs	
Timing of future cash flows	✓

296 The present value of the lease payments at an interest rate of 10% is **$38,328.**

The first payment is on receipt of the machine so the payments are as follows:

	Cash flow	Discount factor	PV
			$
Year 0	8,000	1	8,000
Years 1 − 5	8,000	3.791	30,328
			―――
			38,328

Note: If the payments had been made at the end of the years, then the PV would have been $8,000 × 4.355 = $34,840.

297 D

(100 × 1.063)

298 The payback period of the investment project is **3 years**

(90 ÷ 30) = 3

299

	True
Project A has a higher internal rate of return than Project B	✓
Project A always has a negative NPV	
Project B has higher initial outlay than Project A	
Project B would be preferred if there is a zero cost of capital	✓

300 C

[13 + (6 × 9,362/11,377)]

SECTION 5: CASH MANAGEMENT

THE NATURE OF CASH AND CASH FLOW

301 B

A, C and D will cause a fall. B may increase receivables

302 D

By definition

303 C

Option D is a receipt and options A and B are revenue payments. Option C is the correct answer.

304 D

Options A and B would affect both cash flow and profits. Option C would affect the profits but not the cashflow. Option D is a receipt that would increase cash flow but would not affect profits.

305   The net profit for the business on a cash accounting basis is **$4,000.**

In cash accounting outstanding receivables and payables are ignored and profit is determined by deducting cash payments ($5,000) from cash receipts ($9,000).

306   The working capital cycle for the business is 48 days.

	Days
Raw materials inventory holding period	8
Less: suppliers' payment period	(28)
WIP holding period	4
Finished goods holding period	26
Receivables' collection period	38
Working capital cycle (days)	48

307 A

Supermarkets will have negligible receivables periods and very short inventory holding periods. When they take credit from suppliers it will mean that that the working capital cycle will be negative.

Accountants and construction companies will have large work-in-progress periods which will give them a large working capital cycle. A retailer offering 12 months interest free credit will have a high receivables period and therefore a high working capital cycle.

308 C

A decrease in equity (such as a financial loss) will result in a cash outflow. Reducing long term debt (for example, by repaying a loan) will also result in a cash outflow, as will a reduction in current liabilities (for example, by making a payment to suppliers). A reduction in current assets (such as a reduction in inventory levels) will free up cash for the business and bring in a cash inflow.

CASH BUDGETS

309 B

	True
Pay suppliers early to receive a cash discount	✓
Buy new plant and machinery	
Invest in treasury bills.	✓

The cash surplus is short term and therefore could be utilised by paying creditors early in return for cash discounts or investing in short-term assets such as treasury bills. Buying plant and machinery is a long-term investment and would need a long-term source of finance.

310 Vincent can expect to collect **$20,000** from credit customers during July.

	$
July's sales $25,000 × 20%	5,000
June's sales $20,000 × 60%	12,000
May's sales $30,000 × 10%	3,000
	———
	20,000

311 The budgeted cash collections for March are **$26,600.**

	$
February sales 45% × $28,000	12,600
March sales 50% × $28,000	14,000
	———
	26,600

312 C

	Units
Sales of Z	10,000
Reduction in inventory	2,000
	———
Production	8,000

	Litres
Usage at 2 litres per Z	16,000
Reduction in inventory	5,000
	———
Purchases	11,000
	———

Therefore cash cost is 11,000 × $4 = $44,000.

313 B

Consider sales of $100

Cash receipt in month of sale = 45% × 100 = $45

This is after a discount of 10%, so must represent 45/0.9 = $50 of sales value

Irrecoverable debts = 20% of any month's sales = $20

The receipts in month 2 must be the rest of the sales = 100 – 50 – 20 = $30

314 A

		$
Cash sales 10% of £40,000		4,000
Receivables		
$36,000	× 40% × 96% in 1st month	13,824
	× 50% in 2nd month	18,000
		———
		35,824
		———

315 A

Payment = $(450,000 × 70% + 18,000 + 10,000) = $343,000

316 The cash balance at the end of the month is overdrawn by **$43,000.**

	$
Opening balance	7,000
Receipts from payables	
Re previous month's sales (= opening receivables)	15,000
Re this month's sales (= half this month's sales)	5,000
Payments to payables (= opening payables)	(40,000)
Expenses	(60,000)
	———
Bank overdraft	(43,000)

317 C

Increase in cash balances ($000)   = 100 − 25 − 20 + 20 + 70 + 40

                                      = $175,000

318 C

Firstly, the trend (moving average) for that period needs to be determined. This will be the average sales based on that period, the period before and the period after. This will be [(99 + 68 + 70)/3] = 79.

The seasonal variation is then the difference between the actual sales and this trend = 68 − 79 = − 11.

319 A

320 D

CASH MANAGEMENT

321 D

	$	$
Net profit increase		45,000
Current receivables($1.2/12)	100,000	
New receivables ($1.2 × 1.25/6)	250,000	
Increase	150,000	
Finance cost of increase at 10%		(15,000)
Overall Increase		30,000

322 The level of the proceeds from the investment that have to be set aside as provision for credit liabilities (PCL) is **75%**

323 A

324

	NOT a role of a treasury manager?
Raising finance	
Collecting debts	✓
Investing in short-term assets	
Credit control	✓

325

	Poor security?
Safe combinations are the same for all safes	✓
Keys are kept in a locked cabinet	
Cash counting is not performed in a visible area	
Cash is only banked once a month	✓

INVESTING AND FINANCING

326

	Variable capital value?
Equity shares held in a listed company	✓
Sterling Certificates of Deposits	✓
Unnegotiable local authority deposits	
Instant access deposits	

327 A

328 B

By definition

329 D

The redemption yield is equal to the interest yield added to the redemption gain.

The interest yield on the stock is calculated as a % of market value as follows:

= 6/92 × 100 = 6.5%

If an investor buys the stock now at $92.00 and holds it until maturity, he/she will make a capital gain of 100 − 92 = $8 at redemption (the stock will repay $100 in one year's time for an investment of $98 now). This gives an average annual gain on redemption of $8 for each $92 invested, which is about 8.7% per annum. The approximate redemption yield is therefore the interest yield of 6.5% plus 8.7%, which is about 15.2%.

330 A

The interest yield and redemption yield will vary as the market price varies. The coupon yield should be a constant percentage of the value of the bond.

331 B

This would be an internal influence on cash balances.

332 The overdraft interest charged in March will be **$250**

Interest is only charged on the amount actually overdrawn.

= 1% × $25,000 = $250

SECTION 6: PROVIDING INFORMATION

INFORMATION FOR COMPARISON

333

	Cause of variance?
The storeroom supplying less material than is required by production	
The purchase of cheap material	✓
Poorly maintained machinery	✓
A series of short deliveries	

Cheap material and poorly maintained machinery may lead to increased material usage and therefore an adverse material usage variance.

334 B

A, C and D are not relevant to the use of material.

335 The total variable cost variance for the month was **$6,000** favourable.

According to the CAT 2 examiner, the total variable cost variance is found by looking at the difference between actual variable costs ($46,000 + $39,000 = $85,000) and the original budget. Actual variable costs were $6,000 lower than budget, so the cost variance is favourable.

336 C

A flexible budget is a budget showing costs and revenues at different levels of activity. For variance reporting, actual costs are compared with a flexed budget for the same volume of production and sales. The terms 'flexible' and 'flexed' mean the same, although the term 'flexible budget' might be used to refer to budgets prepared in advance, whereas 'flexed budget' might be used to refer to the preparation at the end of the budget control period of a statement what the expected costs and revenues should have been at the actual volume of sales and production that occurred.

337 A

Feedforward control compares the budgeted outcome with the current best forecast of what actual results will be. For example, suppose that the budgeted sales for the year are 1,000 units. After six months, actual sales for the year to date might be 450 units, and the current estimate of what actual sales will be for the year might be 900 units. Using feedforward control, management will identify a difference of 100 units in sales (1,000 – 900 units) and try to take measures for increasing sales up to the 1,000 target by the end of the year, by selling 550 units in the second half of the year.

338 B

Feedback is information about results that have occurred, comparing actual results with planned results. If control measures are taken to correct any weaknesses or failings revealed by the comparison, the control measures would be a form of feedback control.

339 A

	Fixed budget 100%	Flexed budget 90%	Actual 90%	Variance
	$	$	$	$
Sales	640,000	576,000	570,000	6,000 (A)

340 The total direct labour cost variance due to rate and efficiency factors was **$1,400.**

	Favourable	Adverse
Total direct labour cost variance		✓

Given the question specifies rate and efficiency factors, we compare actual and flexed budget.

	$
7,700 units should cost (× $6)	46,200
They did cost	47,600
Direct labour cost variance	1,400 (A)

341 The total direct material cost variance was **$1,840**

	Favourable	Adverse
Total direct material cost variance		✓

According to the examiner, the total variance should be the difference between actual and original budget, unless specified otherwise.

	$
Original budget (6,500 × $12)	78,000
Actual	79,840
Direct material cost variance	1,840 (A)

342   C

	Fixed budget 100%	Flexed budget 90%	Actual 90%	Variance
	$	$	$	$
Costs:				
Direct costs	250,000	225,000		
Variable overheads	110,000	99,000		
Fixed overheads	220,000	220,000		
Total costs	580,000	544,000	565,000	21,000 (A)

Note: The question specified that the total cost variance should be due to price and usage issues and hence is the difference between actual and flexed budget.

343 B

The size of the variance is relevant. Small variances are unlikely to be worth investigating. Some organisations use a **reporting by exception** system whereby only unusually large results are flagged for management's attention.

The likelihood of a variance being controllable by the manager is relevant. If a variance is likely to be outside the manager's control, there will be no point in spending time and effort investigating it.

The trend in a variance over the course of the year can also be significant. If a variance is getting larger each month, instead of being favourable in one month and adverse in another month, the need for control action might be more urgent.

The factor that should be least likely to affect an investigation is whether the variance is favourable or adverse. If a variance is large and favourable, management might be able to make sure that the favourable variance continues in future months by taking appropriate measures.

344 B

The principle of reporting by exception is that variances are only flagged for management's attention when they exceed a certain limit. For example, material cost variances might only be reported when an adverse variance exceeds 5% of the expected cost and a favourable variance exceeds 10% of the expected cost.

345 C

Budgeted sales for the year are 2,400 units (200 units each month) and the revised forecast is just 2,000 units. This leaves an expected shortfall of 400 units. It also means that to achieve the budget target, sales in the final five months of the year need to be 1,150 units (2,400 − 1,250), which is 400 units more than the current forecast of 750 units (2,000 − 1,250).

Note that with feedback control reporting, the reported cumulative adverse sales variance at the end of month 7, for the year to date would be 150 units (budget for the year to date = 1,400 units, actual sales = 1,250 units).

346

	True?
Feedback and feedforward are both applied in budgetary planning and control.	✓
Feedback is used in the analysis of variances.	✓
Feedforward enables budgeted data for a period to be amended for the next period.	
Feedforward relates to the setting of performance standards.	

Feedback is the comparison of actual results with the budget to date (or with a standard) and an analysis of differences or variances, in order to identify whether control measures are necessary or a revision to the budget is appropriate. Variance analysis is an example of feedback control. **Feedforward** is the forecasting of differences between budgeted and actual outcomes, and taking action if necessary to bring expected results more into line with the budget. Statements 1 and 2 are therefore true, but statements 3 and 4 are not.

347 C

Factors that will affect a decision whether or not to investigate a variance include:

- whether the cause of the variance has not been corrected yet and is controllable

- the cost of investigating the variance and the likely benefits from control action

- whether there is a continuing variance and whether it is getting worse from month to month (i.e. whether there is a continuing trend).

348 B

A flexible budget is a budget that can be adjusted according to the actual level of activity. It recognises, for example, that total variable costs will change if the activity level varies.

349 The total direct material cost variance due to price and usage factors was **$380.**

	Favourable	Adverse
Total direct material cost variance		✓

	$	
8,800 units should cost (× $5)	44,000	
But they did cost	44,380	
	———	
Direct material cost variance	380	(A)
	———	

REPORTING MANAGEMENT INFORMATION

350 C

An ad hoc or special report will be generated occasionally or only once. It will not have a set content and this will vary according to requirements.

Option A describes a routine report. Routine reports contain standard information and are produced regularly, often at set times.

351 D

Management accounting reports should be understandable by non-financial managers. It is totally misguided to think that all managers should be financially literate, and it is important to make sure that reports to non-financial managers are clear and well presented, and that difficult or unusual issues are explained carefully.

352 A

Written methods of communication of all sorts – letters, memos, bulletins, files, circulars – are the norm in many companies. They have the advantage of being less open to misinterpretation because they are in permanent or hard-copy form.

353 B

A component bar chart shows the total sales in any one year. The individual components of each bar should show the sales for the three different products.

354 D

A bar chart is a good way of illustrating total sales month by month. The length of the bar each month is a measure of total sales. The bar can be divided into three parts, to show the amount of sales achieved for each of the three products. This is called a component bar chart.

355 A

356 D

Accounting information is usually confidential and should not be given to anyone without the proper authority.

357 D

Option D alludes to a disadvantage of bar charts. If the bar chart is split into components it is more difficult to see the overall total.

358

	Suitable?
Stacked (compound) bar chart	✓
Line charts	✓
Pie charts	

Pie charts will be least effective to show trends but both of the others will work, although you could argue that the line chart is best.

359 D

Line graphs are very useful to demonstrate trends.

360 C

Line graphs will identify trends as it will be easy to see upward or downward patterns as well as peaks and troughs for seasonality.

361 D

The other graphs/charts rely on some correlation between the variables. A scatter graph is more likely to illustrate a random pattern or non-relationship.

Section 8

MOCK EXAM QUESTIONS

ALL QUESTIONS ARE COMPULSORY AND MUST BE ANSWERED. EACH QUESTION IS WORTH 2 MARKS EACH.

1   **A company maintains a cost ledger for cost accounting purposes. The double entry for direct labour costs is:**

    A   Debit Wages control account, Credit Work-in-progress account

    B   Debit Work-in-progress account, Credit Wages control account

    C   Debit Wages control account, Credit Bank account

    D   Debit Bank account, Credit Wages control account

2   **Which of the following forms of presentation is least useful when comparing how data (such as total sales) has changed over time?**

    A   Pie chart

    B   Bar chart

    C   Table

    D   Line graph

3   **You have been asked to supply the quarterly sales figures for the last six years to the board of directors. What might the appropriate form for communicating such information take?**

    A   Telephone call

    B   Letter

    C   Internal report

    D   Note

4   A particular cost is classified as 'semi-variable'.

    What effect would a 15% reduction in activity have on the unit cost?

    A   Increase by less than 15%

    B   Increase by 15%

    C   Reduce by less than 15%

    D   Remain constant

5 A company produces components for washing machines. Each component has a raw material input of $20 and labour input that costs $10. The company must also pay the rent of the factory totalling $20,000 per annum, production supervisor's costs of $25,000 per annum and the managing director's salary of $35,000 per annum. The budgeted output is 10,000 units per annum.

The fixed production cost is:

A $45,000

B $75,000

C $80,000

D $115,000

6 A particular cost is classified as being fixed.

If activity increases by 10% what will happen to the cost per unit?

A   Increases

B   Reduces but not in proportion to the change in activity

C   Reduces in proportion to the change in activity

D   Remains constant

The following information relates to questions 7 and 8.

The re-order level of Material X is 1,200 kg and the order quantity is 600 kg. Lead times and usage are as follows:

Lead time:	minimum	2 weeks
	average	3 weeks
	maximum	4 weeks
Usage:	minimum	200 kg per week
	average	300 kg per week
	maximum	400 kg per week

---

7 **What is the maximum inventory control level of Material X?**

A   1,400 kg

B   1,600 kg

C   1,700 kg

D   1,900 kg

8 **What is the minimum inventory control level of Material X?**

A   Nil

B   300 kg

C   500 kg

D   700 kg

The following information relates to questions 9 and 10.

The inventory record for Component RST for the month of June showed:

Day	Receipts	Value	Issues
		$	
Opening balance	200	2,500	
4	800	10,200	
11	1,200	15,360	
18	2,700	35,100	
19			2,100
25	2,500	32,750	
30			1,800

9   **Using the FIFO method of pricing issues, the cost of issues during the month was:**

A $49,725

B $49,920

C $50,160

D $50,700

10   **Using the LIFO method of pricing issues, what is the value of inventory held at 30 June?**

A $41,395

B $43,275

C $45,030

D $50,880

11   **If a company is using the FIFO method for material issues at a time when material prices are rising, this will mean which of the following?**

1   Profits will be higher than if LIFO was used

2   Profits will be higher than if weighted average pricing was used

3   The closing inventory valuation will be lower than if LIFO is used

A   All of the statements are true

B   Statements 1 and 2 are true, statement 3 is false

C   Statements 2 and 3 are true, statement 1 is false

D   All of the statements are false

12 A company makes a product for which the standard hour is 0.2. The budgeted production hours for a given week were 10,500. During the week the production staff were able to produce 1,980 units of product. Actual wage costs were $65,000 and idle time was recorded as $1,625. The wage rate was $6.50 per hour.

The efficiency ratio was therefore:

A   94.3%

B   97.5%

C   99.0%

D   101.5%

13 **Which of the following are disadvantages of using pie charts to represent information?**

1   Exact values are difficult to determine

2   When values are similar differences are hard to determine

A   1 only

B   2 only

C   1 and 2

D   Neither

14 The costs associated with labour turnover can be classified as 'preventative' costs or 'replacement' costs.

Which of the following is a preventative cost?

A   Provision of leisure facilities for employees

B   Lower productivity of new employees

C   Increased wastage of raw materials

D   Training costs for new employees

15 Consider the following statements, regarding the reapportionment of service cost centre overheads to production cost centres, where reciprocal services exist:

1   The direct method results in costs being reapportioned between service cost centres.

2   If the direct method is used, the order in which the service cost centre overheads are reapportioned is irrelevant.

3   The step down method results in costs being reapportioned between service cost centres.

4   If the step down method is used, the order in which the service cost centre overheads are reapportioned is irrelevant.

Which statement(s) is/are correct?

A   1, 2 and 4

B   1, 3 and 4

C   2 only

D   2 and 3

16   **Which of the following statements about cost and management accounting are true?**

   1   Cost accounting cannot be used to provide inventory valuations for external financial reporting.

   2   There is a legal requirement to prepare management accounts.

   3   The format of management accounts may vary from one business to another.

   4   Management accounting provides information to help management make business decisions.

   A   1 and 2

   B   1 and 4

   C   2 and 3

   D   3 and 4

17   **Which of the following are features of an efficient and effective cost coding system?**

   1   Codes need to be complex to include all items.

   2   Each code must have a combination of alphabetic and numeric characters.

   3   Codes for a particular type of item should be consistent in length and structure.

   A   1 only

   B   3 only

   C   1 and 2

   D   2 and 3

18   A company has two production cost centres – A and B. The following information is available:

Cost centre	A	B
Budgeted production overhead	$350,000	$525,000
Budgeted direct labour hours	10,000	50,000
Budgeted machine hours	40,000	5,000
Actual overhead cost	$325,000	$512,000
Actual labour hours	8,000	52,000
Actual machine hours	42,000	8,000
Overhead recovery rate	$8.75 per machine hour	$10.50 per direct labour hour

   The total over-recovery of overheads was

   A $38,000

   B $76,500

   C $114,500

   D $0

The following information relates to questions 19 to 21.

A company manufactures a single product which it sells for $35 per unit. The planned output for 20X6 was 6,000 units. The unit product cost comprises:

	$
Direct labour	8.50
Direct material	2.50
Variable overhead	
1.5 hours × $2.50/hour	3.75
Fixed overhead	
1.5 hours × $8.00/hour	12.00
	─────
	26.75
	─────

19 **If the company uses a marginal costing approach to prepare its profit statement, what would be the amount of total contribution shown in the budget statement for 20X6 (assuming no closing and opening inventory will be held)?**

   A $49,500

   B $75,000

   C $121,500

   D $144,000

20 **If the forecast inventory level at 31 December was 360 units and it was valued on the basis of absorption cost, what would be the value of inventory held on this date?**

   A $3,960

   B $5,310

   C $9,630

   D $12,600

21 **What would be the budgeted profit for the year based on the marginal costing technique (assuming production is 6,000 units and closing inventory is 360 units)?**

   A $42,210

   B $72,680

   C $108,900

   D $150,870

22 **Which of the following is not a characteristic of service costing?**

   A   Normal losses

   B   No inventory held

   C   Composite cost units

   D   No physical product

23 There are two production cost centres and two service cost centres in a factory. Production overheads have been allocated and apportioned to cost centres and now require re-apportionment from service cost centres to production cost centres. Relevant details are:

	Service cost centre A	Service cost centre B
Total overhead	$160,000	$85,000
% to Production cost centre X	25	75
% to Production cost centre Y	55	25
% to Service Cost Centre B	20	

What is the total re-apportionment to Production cost centre Y?

A $103,750

B $109,250

C $117,250

D $125,550

24 A company is preparing a quote for Job 265. The costs and other related information include:

	$
Raw materials	325
Direct labour	648
Production overhead	$2.50 per labour hour
Administrative overhead	10% of production cost
Profit margin	25% of selling price

Note: Direct labour is paid $7.20 per hour.

The sales price of Job 265 to the customer would have been:

A $1,506.09

B $1,532.16

C $1,647.25

D $1,757.07

25 Costs totalling $4,250 were incurred in a process in a period. 80 units of output were rejected and destroyed in the period, 20 units more than allowed for as a normal loss, leaving 420 units of good production to be transferred to finished goods.

What is the amount written off as abnormal loss (to the nearest $)?

A $170

B $177

C $193

D $202

26 A company operates a process costing system. The process is expected to lose 10% of input and this can be sold for $0.45 per kg.

Inputs for the month were:

Direct materials	2,500 kg at a total cost of $4,425
Direct labour	$5,250 for the period

There is no opening or closing work-in-progress in the period. Actual output was 2,150 kg.

What is the valuation of the output?

A $9,055.50

B $9,137.50

C $9,245.00

D $9,675.00

27 A firm uses job costing. Details of the three jobs worked on during a period are:

	Job BA	Job DC	Job FE
	$	$	$
Opening work-in-progress	22,760	3,190	–
Direct materials in the period	4,620	11,660	14,335
Direct labour in the period	12,125	10,520	7,695

Overheads are absorbed at 40% of prime cost in each period. Jobs DC and FE remained incomplete at the end of the period.

What is the value of the closing work-in-progress?

A $61,894

B $65,084

C $66,360

D $68,952

28 Consider the following statements relating to process costing:

Statement 1: normal losses are credited to the process account at the cost per unit incurred on normal production.

Statement 2: abnormal gains are debited to the process account at the cost per unit incurred on normal production.

Which statement(s) is/are true?

A   Both statements are true

B   Neither statement is true

C   Statement 1 only is true

D   Statement 2 only is true

29 A company manufactures and sells four products. Details are as follows:

	Product			
	P	Q	R	S
	$	$	$	$
Contribution per unit	16.0	14.5	17.6	19.0
Net profit per unit	4.6	4.8	5.2	5.0
Contribution per machine hour	5.0	4.8	4.4	3.8
Net profit per machine hour	1.4	1.6	1.3	1.0

Machine hours available in the next period will not be sufficient to meet production requirements. There are no product-specific fixed costs.

What should be the order of priority for production in order to maximise profit?

A Product P, Product Q, Product R, Product S

B Product Q, Product P, Product R, Product S

C Product R, Product S, Product Q, Product P

D Product S, Product R, Product P, Product Q

30 **What is a by-product?**

A A product that has insignificant saleable value compared with the joint products

B A product that has no saleable value

C A product that can be further processed

D A waste product that has to be disposed of at a cost

31 A company has incurred development costs of $25,000 to date on a proposed new product. Further costs of $18,000 would be required to complete the development of the product.

In deciding whether to continue with the new product development which of the following is correct regarding development costs?

	Sunk cost	Incremental cost
A	$0	$43,000
B	$18,000	$25,000
C	$25,000	$18,000
D	$43,000	$0

32 **A company is considering whether to purchase an investment that would earn an income of $18,000 in perpetuity. The company would want a return of at least 12%. What is the maximum price it should be prepared to pay for the investment?**

A $150,000

B $185,000

C $200,000

D $216,000

33 An investment project has net present values as follows:

Discount rate 11% per annum: net present value $35,170 positive.

Discount rate 15% per annum: net present value $6,040 positive.

What is the best estimate of the internal rate of return?

A   14.5%

B   15.8%

C   19.5%

D   19.8%

34 A company is proposing to launch a new product. Incremental net cash inflows of $36,000 per annum for five years are expected, starting at Time 1.

An existing machine, with a net book value of $85,000, would be used to manufacture the new product. The machine could otherwise be sold now, Time 0, for $60,000. The machine, if used for the manufacture of the new product, would be depreciated on a straight-line basis over five years, starting at Time 1.

What are the relevant amounts that should be used, at Time 0 and Time 1, in the discounted cash flow appraisal of the project?

	Time 0	Time 1
A	$0	$19,000
B	$0	$24,000
C	($60,000)	$36,000
D	($85,000)	$36,000

35 The labour requirements for a special contract are 85 skilled labour hours paid $15 per hour.

At present skilled labour is in short supply, and all such labour used on this contract will be at the expense of other work which generates a contribution of $18 per hour (after charging labour costs). The relevant cost of labour for the special contract is:

A $1,275

B $1,530

C $2,805

D   Nil

36 **Which of the following MUST be paid each year:**

A   Interest on an unused overdraft

B   Coupon interest on bonds

C   Dividends on ordinary shares

D   All of the above

37 Production costs have been estimated at two levels of output:

	50,000 units	52,000 units	55,000 units
Prime costs	$430,000	$480,000	$473,000
Overheads	$330,000	$335,000	$339,000

What are the estimated production costs per unit at an output level of 54,000 units?

A $14.76

B $14.84

C $15.20

D $17.00

38 Celtic Ltd budgeted to make sales of $1,000, $800 and $1,500 in its first three months of operation.

35% of its sales are expected to be for cash and 15% of total sales will also be collected in the same month by offering a 10% discount; 30% will be collected in the following month, and the remainder the month after that.

How much cash did Celtic Ltd budget to receive in its third month of operation?

A $1,115.00

B $1,167.50

C $1,190.00

D $1,500.00

39 **4% Treasury stock is currently valued at $98 and is redeemable in one year's time. What is the redemption yield?**

A   2%

B   4%

C   6%

D   8%

40 **Which of the following is not typically a feature of service costing?**

A   Allocating costs between fixed and variable elements

B   Accurate time recording

C   Accuracy in valuing work in progress

D   Unique nature of the work

41 **A floating charge is most likely to be placed over which of the following:**

A   A machine

B   Inventory

C   An overdraft

D   Bank payments

42   ABC has produced the following sales forecast:

	$000
January	750
February	760
March	770
April	780
May	790
June	800

Currently 20% of customers pay in cash. Of the credit customers (excluding those who become irrecoverable debts), 60% pay in one month, 30% pay in two months and 10% in three months. Irrecoverable debts are 2%. This payment pattern is expected to continue.

What are the forecast cash receipts in April?

A $755,760

B $696,960

C $814,400

D $604,000

43   **Matching revenues to the period in which the benefit is derived, irrespective of when receipt actually occurs, is an example of what?**

A   Cash accounting

B   Good banking procedures

C   Good treasury management

D   The accruals concept

44   A business makes two products, A and B, for which the budgeted and actual direct material costs for a particular period are as follows.

	Product	Units of production	Cost
Budget	A	11,000 units	$55,000
	B	22,500 units	$45,000
Actual	A	9,750 units	$51,300
	B	23,800 units	$46,400

What was the total direct material cost variance based on price/usage factors for the period?

A $3,750 Adverse

B $1,350 Adverse

C $2,300 Favourable

D $2,450 Favourable

45 The following budgeted and actual results apply to a business operation:

	Budget	Actual
	$	$
Sales revenue	300,000	240,000
Direct materials	70,000	61,300
Direct labour	50,000	42,100
Fixed overheads	90,000	89,000
Total costs	210,000	192,400
Profit	90,000	47,600

Actual sales by volume came to 85% of the budgeted volume.

What was the total cost variance for the period?

A $17,600 Favourable

B $13,900 Adverse

C $6,400 Adverse

D $400 Adverse

46 **Which of the following might explain an adverse direct labour cost variance?**

1 Working overtime

2 Idle time

3 Poor productivity

A Reasons 1 and 2 only

B Reasons 1 and 3 only

C Reasons 2 and 3 only

D Reason 3 only

47 The budgeted and actual results for a business that makes and sells a single product are as follows.

	Budget	Actual
Sales (units)	10,000	9,000
	$	$
Sales revenue	150,000	125,000

What was the sales volume variance?

A $10,000 Adverse

B $15,000 Adverse

C $20,000 Adverse

D $25,000 Adverse

48   The budgeted expenditure for a department is $30,000 each month, or $360,000 for the year. A performance report at the end of the third month showed the following information:

	Budget	Actual
	$	$
Expenditure in the month	30,000	34,200
Cumulative expenditure, year to date	90,000	98,750

Budgeted expenditure for the year	$360,000
Current forecast of annual expenditure	$425,000

Which of the following items of information is relevant for feedforward control?

A   Monthly expenditure needs to be reduced by $4,200 to get back to budgeted spending levels

B   Expenditure has to be reduced by $8,750 to get back to budgeted spending levels

C   Expenditure is expected to exceed budget for the year by $65,000

D   Expenditure is expected to exceed budget for the year by $73,750

49   **A business has a seasonal sales pattern. Management reports are produced each month. Which of the following comparisons would be suitable for control purposes?**

1   Comparison with sales in the corresponding month last year

2   Budgeted sales for the month

3   Comparison with previous month's sales in the current year

A   1 and 2 only

B   2 only

C   2 and 3 only

D   1, 2 and 3

50   **Action taken in response to differences between the budgeted and actual performance in a period is an example of which of the following?**

A   Feedback control

B   Feedforward control

C   Flexed budgeting

D   Budgetary planning

Section 9

MOCK EXAM ANSWERS

1   B

Total labour costs would be debited to the Wages control account and credited to the Bank account. Wages would then be analysed as direct and indirect with direct costs being debited to the WIP account and indirect costs being debited to the Production overhead account.

2   A

It is very difficult to portray such information easily using a pie chart. The other methods can all do this much more easily.

3   C

This will need more formal communication than a note or telephone call and the directors are likely to want to view the figures in more detail. A letter will be too slow and costly, so an informal report is likely to be the best device to use.

4   A

5   A

Raw material and labour are variable costs and the managing director's salary would not be classified as a production cost.

6   B

If fixed cost is $100, then the cost per unit for 10 units is $10 per unit. If activity increases by 10% to 11 units the fixed cost per unit is now ($100/11) $9.09. This is a reduction of .91/10 = 9.1%

7   A

Maximum inventory control level = ROQ + ROL – (Minimum demand × Minimum lead time)

= 600 + 1,200 – (2 × 200)

= 1,400 kg

8   B

Minimum inventory control level = ROL – (Average demand × Average lead time)

= 1,200 – (3 × 300)

= 300 kg

9   C

Using FIFO 3,900 units are issued and these should be valued at the earliest prices.

Value   = $2,500 + $10,200 + $15,360 + (1,700 × $35,100/2,700)

= $50,160

10   C

Using LIFO the issue on 19/6 would be 2,100 units at $13. Leaving 600 at $13

The issue on 30 June would be 1,800 at $13.10, leaving 700 at $13.10.

The value of the closing inventory would therefore be:

Opening balance		$2,500
4/6 Receipt		$10,200
11/6 Receipt		$15,360
18/6 Receipt	600 × $13	$7,800
25/6 Receipt	700 × $13.10	$9,170
		———
		$45,030

11   B

Using FIFO issues are made at the earliest (lowest) prices. Therefore profits will be higher than if either LIFO or weighted average pricing were used. Inventory will be valued at later (higher) prices so will have a higher valuation than if LIFO was used.

12   D

The actual output in standard hours = 1,980 / 0.2 = 9,900

Actual hours worked = $\dfrac{\$65,000 - \$1,625}{\$6.50}$ = 9,750

The efficiency ratio = 9,900/9,750 × 100% = 101.5%

13   C

14   A

15   D

16   D

17 B

18 B

Overhead absorbed in cost centre A = 42,000 × $8.75 = $367,500

Overhead absorbed in cost centre B = 52,000 × $10.50 = $546,000

	A	B	Total
Overhead absorption			
Cost centre A	367,500		
Cost centre B		546,000	
Total			$913,500
Overhead incurred			
Cost centre A	325,000		
Cost centre B		512,000	
Total			$837,000
Over-recovery of overhead			$76,500

19 C

Sales 6,000 × $35	$210,000
Less variable cost 6,000 × $14.75	($88,500)
Contribution	$121,500

20 C

360 × $26.75 = $9,630

21 A

Sales must be 6,000 − 360 = 5,640 units

	$
Sales (5,640 × $35)	197,400
Cost of sales (5,640 × $14.75)	(83,190)
Contribution	114,210
Fixed costs (6,000 × $12)	72,000
Profit	42,210

22 A

A service industry is characterised by having no physical output and therefore no inventory is held. Composite cost units such as cost per tonne-km are common. Normal losses are a feature of process costing.

23   C

	X	Y	A	B
			160,000	85,000
Re-apportion A	40,000	88,000	(160,000)	32,000
Re-apportion B	87,750	29,250		(117,000)
		117,250		

24   D

	$
Raw materials	325
Direct labour	648
Production overhead	
$648/$7.2 = 90 hours at $2.50	225
	1,198
Administration overhead	119.8
	1,317.8
Profit margin 25/75 × Full cost	439.27
	1,757.07

25   C

{[$4,250 ÷ (420 units good output + 20 units abnormal loss)] × 20 units}

26   B

Input	2,500
Normal loss	250
	2,250
Actual output	2,150
Abnormal loss	100

Cost per unit = $\dfrac{\$4,425 + \$5,250 - (250 \times \$0.45)}{2,250}$ = $4.25

Output value = $4.25 × 2,150 = $9,137.50

27   B

[($44,210 × 1.4) + $3,190]

28   D

29   A

30   **A**

31   **C**

32   **A**

$18,000/0.12 = $150,000

33   **B**

{11% + [4% × ($35,170/$29,130)]}

34   **C**

35   **C**

		$
Basic pay	85 × $15	1,275
Lost contribution	85 × $18	1,530
		2,805

36   **B**

Coupon interest on bonds must be paid. Dividend payments are discretionary. No interest is paid on unused overdrafts.

37   **B**

($52,000 ÷ 5,000 units) + {[($760,000 − (50,000 units × $10.40/unit)] ÷ 54,000 units}

38   **B**

	$
Cash sales in month 3: (35% of $1,500)	525.00
Cash from credit sales in month 3: (15% of $1,500, less 10%)	202.50
Cash from credit sales in month 2: (30% of $800)	240.00
Cash from credit sales in month 1: (20% of $1,000)	200.00
	1,167.50

39 C

The redemption yield is equal to the interest yield added to the redemption gain.

The interest yield on the stock is calculated as a % of market value as follows:

$= 4/98 \times 100 = 4.1\%$

If an investor buys the stock now at $92.00 and holds it until maturity, he/she will make a capital gain of $100 - 98 = \$2$ at redemption (the stock will repay $100 in one year's time for an investment of $98 now). This gives an average annual gain on redemption of $2 for each $98 invested, which is about 2.0% per annum.

The approximate redemption yield is therefore the interest yield of 4.1% plus 2%, which is about 6%.

40 D

41 B

42 A

The customer cannot be asked for immediate payment once a bill of exchange has been accepted.

		Cash received
		$
April sales	20% × $780,000	156,000
March sales	80% × 0.98 × $770,000 × 60%	362,208
February sales	80% × 0.98 × $760,000 × 30%	178,752
January sales	80% × 0.98 × $750,000 × 10%	58,800
		————
		755,760

43 D

44 B

The budgeted direct material cost for A is $55,000/11,000 units = $5 per unit.

The budgeted direct material cost for B is $45,000/22,500 units = $2 per unit.

	$
9,750 units of A should cost (× $5)	48,750
23,800 units of B should cost (× $2)	47,600
	————
Together they should cost	96,350
They did cost ($51,300 + $46,400)	97,700
	————
Direct material cost variance	1,350 (A)
	————

45   A

For this paper, the total cost variance is the difference between actual and original budget, unless the exam specifies that it should only incorporate price/rate and usage/efficiency factors.

46   D

The cost of overtime premium and the cost of idle time are treated as indirect labour costs, and so would not affect the calculation of the direct labour cost variance. Poor productivity/efficiency means that it takes longer to produce the work than expected; therefore unit costs for direct labour will be higher than expected.

47   B

Flexed budget for actual sales = 9,000 units × $15 = $135,000

The sales volume variance is the difference between the original budget and the flexed budget for actual sales.

Sales volume variance = $(150,000 – 135,000) = $15,000 Adverse

48   C

Feedforward control is based on a comparison of the budget for a given period and the current forecast of what actual results will be. Here, the budget is $360,000 and the current revised forecast is now $425,000, which is $65,000 higher. This includes the excess spending of $8,750 for the year to date. Comparisons of actual spending and budgeted spending for month 3 and for the year to date are examples of feedback control information.

49   A

Useful comparisons for control purposes are sales in the month compared with sales in the same month last year, and sales in the month compared with budgeted sales for the month. However, a comparison with sales in the previous month of the same year would not be useful control information, because sales are seasonal and so will fluctuate from one month to the next during the course of the year.

50   A

This is an example of feedback control. The action may be taken to correct deviations or to revise the budget if appropriate.

FOUNDATIONS IN ACCOUNTANCY

Managing Costs and Finance

Specimen Exam applicable from June 2014

Time allowed: 2 hours

ALL 50 questions are compulsory and MUST be attempted.

Do NOT open this paper until instructed by the supervisor.

This question paper must not be removed from the examination hall.

The Association of Chartered Certified Accountants

Paper MA2

ALL 50 questions are compulsory and MUST be attempted

Please use the space provided on the inside cover of the Candidate Answer Booklet to indicate your chosen answer to each multiple choice question.
Each question is worth 2 marks.

1 **Which costing method would be MOST suitable for an accountancy firm?**

    A   Contract costing
    B   Job costing
    C   Batch costing
    D   Process costing

2 **Which of the following statements, about establishing the trend of a time series, is/are TRUE?**

    (1) Where the time series is approximately linear, the line of best fit can be estimated on a scatter graph
    (2) Where the time series is not approximately linear, moving averages can be calculated

    A   1 only
    B   2 only
    C   Both 1 and 2
    D   Neither 1 nor 2

3 Four vertical lines have been labelled G, H, J and K at different levels of activity on the following profit-volume chart:

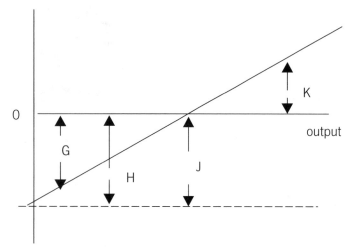

Which line represents the total contribution at that level of activity?

    A   Line G
    B   Line H
    C   Line J
    D   Line K

4   The following is a list of statements relating to terms used in process costing.

Which TWO items in the following list relate to the term 'by product'?

(1) Has low sales value relative to joint products
(2) Accounted for by crediting the net realisable value to the work-in-progress account
(3) Equivalent units of output are less than the actual good units of output
(4) Charged with a share of joint production costs

A   1 and 2
B   1 and 3
C   2 and 4
D   3 and 4

5   The following data are available for product X.

	Period Budget	Period Actual
Sales units	5,000	5,200
	$	$
Sales revenue	50,000	57,200*
Manufacturing cost	30,000	31,200

What is the sales price variance?

A $5,200 adverse
B $5,000 favourable
C $5,200 favourable
D $7,200 favourable

6   A company orders a particular raw material in order quantities of 250 units. No safety inventory is held, the inventory holding cost is $3 per unit per annum and the annual demand is 2,500 units.

What is the total annual inventory holding cost of the material?

A $375
B $750
C $3,750
D $7,500

7   A company has two production cost centres, Cutting and Finishing.

The overheads and operating hours for the two cost centres are:

Cutting:	$210,000	60,000 machine hours	4,000 labour hours
Finishing:	$200,000	5,000 machine hours	14,000 labour hours

From the information given what should be the basis for overhead absorption?

A   Both cost centres should be based on machine hours
B   Both cost centres should be based on labour hours
C   Based on machine hours for Cutting and labour hours for Finishing
D   Based on labour hours for Cutting and machine hours for Finishing

8 A company uses the production units method to depreciate the machinery in its factory. A machine that cost $166,200 has an estimated residual value of $5,000 at the end of its six-year useful operating life.

Output from the machine is estimated as 124,000 units over the six years. 15% of the total output will be manufactured in each of Years 1, 2 and 3 with 20% of the total in Years 4 and 5.

What is the total depreciation of the machine in Year 4?

A $33,240
B $32,240
C $37,929
D $39,106

9 12,000 kg of materials, costing $86,090, were input to a manufacturing process in a period during which conversion costs totalled $39,320. Losses in the period were 960 kg with no saleable value. The normal loss is 10% of input.

What was the total manufacturing cost per kg of expected output (to two decimal places of $)?

A $9·68
B $10·45
C $11·36
D $11·61

10 Which of the following may be included in the cost accounts but would be excluded from the financial accounts?

A Depreciation of equipment
B Distribution expenses
C Factory manager's salary
D Notional rent

11 A company is evaluating a project that requires 400 kg of raw material X. The company has 150 kg of X in stock that was purchased six months ago for $55 per kg. The company no longer has any use for X. The inventory of X could be sold for $40 per kg. The current purchase price for X is $53 per kg.

What is the total relevant cost of raw material X for the project?

A $21,200
B $21,500
C $19,250
D $13,250

12 Dipton have apportioned their indirect costs as shown below:

	DEPT A	DEPT B	DEPT C	DEPT D
Rent and rates ($)	10,000	15,000	45,000	12,500
Heat and lighting ($)	15,000	25,000	25,000	20,000
Administration ($)	15,000	35,000	35,000	35,000
Premises insurance ($)	20,000	15,000	15,000	12,500
Total ($)	60,000	90,000	120,000	80,000
Hours worked:				
Direct labour	10,000	15,000	12,500	10,000
Machine	5,000	20,000	15,000	12,500

If direct labour hours are used to absorb the indirect costs, which department will have the highest hourly absorption rate?

A Department A
B Department B
C Department C
D Department D

13 Two statements follow about the purpose of an email system:

1. The purpose of an email system is to send and receive data a computer can work with.
2. The purpose of an email system is to send and receive messages quickly and cheaply.

Are the statements true or false?

A Both statements are false
B Both statements are true
C Statement 1 is false and Statement 2 is true
D Statement 1 is true and Statement 2 is false

14 In a transport business, unit costs are calculated per tonne/kilometre. The following data is available:

Average load (tonnes)	Average distance (kilometres)	Number of journeys
4	40	10
5	60	12
6	65	8

Total costs were $34,295.

What was the cost per tonne/kilometre (to two decimal places of $)?

A $0·46
B $1·34
C $4·12
D $13·86

15 **Which of the following are objectives of cash budgeting?**

(1) To anticipate cash shortages and surpluses
(2) To enable necessary funds to be made available
(3) To monitor trade receivables

A 1 and 2 only
B 1 and 3 only
C 2 and 3 only
D 1, 2 and 3

16 **Which of the following describes a flexible budget?**

A A budget that is adjusted to the actual level of activity achieved
B A budget that can be varied by any circumstances
C A budget that is adjusted for inflation
D A budget to allow new product development

17 **Which of the following formulae can be used for calculating labour efficiency ratio?**

A Actual hours ÷ standard hours of actual output
B Budgeted hours ÷ actual hours
C Standard hours of actual output ÷ actual hours
D Standard hours of actual output ÷ budgeted hours

18 In Year 1 a company incurred the following indirect costs:

Heat and lighting	$35,000
Rent and rates	$45,000

These costs are apportioned to Department A and Department B on the basis of floor area occupied. A occupies 10,000 square metres and B occupies 5,000 square metres. In Year 2 the indirect costs will rise by 20% and the size of the building will be increased by one third. Department C will occupy the new area.

In Year 2 how much of the indirect costs will be apportioned to Department B?

A $20,000
B $24,000
C $32,000
D $48,000

19 **Which of the following items are treated differently in cash accounting compared with accruals accounting?**

(1) Depreciation
(2) Sales income
(3) Expenditure on materials

A 1 only
B 1 and 2 only
C 2 and 3 only
D 1, 2 and 3

20 A hotel had total costs of $1,500,000 for a period. There were a total of 120,000 occupied bed-nights in the period.

What is the cost per service unit (to two decimal places)?

A $0·08
B $3·42
C $12·50
D $29·20

21 **Which TWO of the following tasks related to cash handling need to be separated (i.e. the same employee cannot perform both tasks), in order to prevent fraud from being committed and concealed?**

(1) Access to liquid assets
(2) Filing of procedures
(3) Investment of surplus funds
(4) Recording of transactions

A   1 and 3
B   1 and 4
C   2 and 4
D   3 and 4

22 A company manufactures a single product which is sold for $70·00 per unit. Unit costs are

	$/Unit
Variable production	29·50
Fixed production	21·00
Variable selling	4·80
Fixed selling	9·00

20,000 units of the product were manufactured in a period during which 19,700 units were sold.

Using marginal costing, what was the total contribution made in the period?

A $703,290
B $714,000
C $384,150
D $390,000

23 A company planned to produce 4,000 units of Product X during a particular year and budgeted its fixed production overheads for the year at $20,000. During the year it actually produced 4,200 units of Product X and it incurred fixed production overheads of $21,840. A predetermined fixed production overhead absorption rate per unit is applied.

Which of the following statements is true?

A   Fixed overheads were under-absorbed by $840
B   Fixed overheads were over-absorbed by $840
C   Fixed overheads were over-absorbed by $1,000
D   Fixed overheads were under-absorbed by $1,840

[P.T.O.

24 A firm has discovered that the cost of a raw material will increase.

If nothing else changes what is the effect of this on margin of safety and breakeven point?

A   The margin of safety will decrease and the breakeven point will increase
B   The margin of safety will increase and the breakeven point will increase
C   The margin of safety will decrease and the breakeven point will decrease
D   The margin of safety will increase and the breakeven point will decrease

25 **Which of the following unbudgeted events could lead to a favourable cash flow variance?**

A   Extended credit given to customers
B   Reduced depreciation charges
C   Extended credit given by suppliers
D   Taking advantage of early settlement discounts offered by suppliers

26 The cost accountant in a factory has set out the following summary data for the last two periods:

	Period 1	Period 2
Total production costs ($)	47,328	51,652
Output (units)	2,400	2,900

What is the BEST estimate of the variable production costs per unit of output (to two decimal places)?

A $17·81
B $19·72
C $18·68
D $ 8·65

27 The occupancy rates for a hotel over a two year period are shown below:

| | Year 1 | | | | Year 2 | | | |
	Qtr 1	Qtr 2	Qtr 3	Qtr 4	Qtr 1	Qtr 2	Qtr 3	Qtr 4
Percentage of bedrooms occupied	60%	75%	90%	60%	65%	85%	95%	55%

Which of the following statements is correct?

A   The occupancy rate for Year 1 is higher than Year 2 for quarters 3 and 4
B   The occupancy rate for Year 2 is higher than Year 1 for quarters 1, 2 and 3
C   The occupancy rate for Year 2 is higher than Year 1 for all four quarters
D   The occupancy rate for Year 1 is higher than Year 2 for quarters 1, 2 and 3

28 The following information relates to Product X for Month 1:

Opening inventory	Nil
Production	900 units
Sales	800 units

If marginal costing rather than absorption costing is used what is the effect on profit and inventory valuation?

A   Profit higher   Inventory valuation higher
B   Profit higher   Inventory valuation lower
C   Profit lower   Inventory valuation higher
D   Profit lower   Inventory valuation lower

8

29 All sales of a company are on credit. Budgets for a period include:

Sales	$724,000
Opening trade receivables	$206,900
Closing trade receivables	$241,600

$4,360 of the opening trade receivables are budgeted to be written off as bad debts during the period.

What are the budgeted cash receipts from sales in the period?

A $684,940
B $689,300
C $754,340
D $758,700

30 The following cost details relate to a single product manufactured by Business X:

	Per Unit
Direct materials (5 kg)	$30
Direct labour (11 hours)	$77
Production overheads	$45

During the next period direct labour will be restricted to 340,000 hours and only 140,000 kg of material will be available. Demand is expected to be 30,000 units.

What will be the limiting factor for the next period?

A   Material only
B   Labour only
C   Material and labour
D   Neither material nor labour

31 A company has calculated that its production volume ratio is 103·5% and that its efficiency ratio is 90·0%.

What is the capacity utilisation ratio (to the nearest whole number)?

A   115
B   93
C   194
D   94

32 **When is the breakeven point achieved?**

A   When the level of contribution is equal to total costs
B   When the total variable costs are equal to total contributions
C   When the total variable costs are equal to total fixed costs
D   When the total contribution is equal to total fixed costs

33 Which TWO of the following statements relating to relevant cost concepts in decision making are correct?

(1) Materials can never have an opportunity cost whereas labour can
(2) The annual depreciation charge is not a relevant cost
(3) Fixed costs would have a relevant cost element if a decision causes a change in their total expenditure
(4) Materials already held in inventory never contribute to relevant cost

A   1 and 3
B   1 and 4
C   2 and 3
D   3 and 4

34 The following data relates to a raw material:

Date		Units	Unit Price $	Value $
1 Jan	Balance b/f	100	5·00	500·00
3 Mar	Issue	40		
4 Jun	Receipt	50	5·50	275·00
6 Jun	Receipt	50	6·00	300·00
9 Sept	Issue	70		

If the LIFO method of pricing is used, what is the value of the issue on 9 September?

A $350
B $395
C $410
D $420

35 A firm with a cost of capital of 12% per annum is considering investing $20,000 now in order to receive 10 annual sums of $4,000 (commencing in one year's time). The annuity factor for 12% over 10 years is 5·65.

What is the net present value of the investment?

A $2,600 positive
B $2,600 negative
C $20,000 positive
D $22,600 positive

36 A company operates a piecework payment scheme. Workers receive $0·60 for each unit produced. However the company guarantees that each worker will receive at least $45 per day.

Shown below is the number of units produced by worker A during a recent week:

Day	Monday	Tuesday	Wednesday	Thursday	Friday
Units produced	90	70	75	60	90

What are worker A's earnings for the week?

A $225
B $243
C $231
D $456

37 An investment made now would yield $15,972 in three years if compound interest is earned at an annual rate of 10%.

What is the amount of the investment now?

A $12,000
B $13,200
C $10,909·10
D $11,643·59

38 A company manufactures and sells four products. Sales demand cannot be met owing to a shortage of skilled labour. Details of the four products are:

	Product A	Product B	Product C	Product D
Sales demand (units)	1,500	2,000	1,800	1,900
Contribution ($/unit)	2·80	2·60	1·90	2·40
Contribution/sales (%)	30	40	50	45
Skilled labour (hours/unit)	1·4	1·2	0·9	1·0

In what order should the products be made in order to maximise profit?

A   Product A, Product B, Product D, Product C
B   Product B, Product D, Product C, Product A
C   Product C, Product D, Product B, Product A
D   Product D, Product B, Product C, Product A

39 **What is an investment centre?**

A   Part of a business involved in financial services
B   Part of a business that utilises equipment and machinery
C   Part of a business where management are responsible both for revenues and for operating costs
D   Part of a business where management are responsible for decisions regarding the purchase of non-current assets

40 **When communicating written information, which of the following determine(s) the choice of method used?**

(1) Comparative cost
(2) Degree of confidentiality
(3) Speed of delivery

A   1 only
B   3 only
C   1 and 2 only
D   1, 2 and 3

41 **Which of the following would appear as an item in a cash budget?**

(1) Depreciation of a non-current asset
(2) Loss on sale of a non-current asset
(3) Payment for the purchase of a non-current asset

A   3 only
B   1 and 2 only
C   2 and 3 only
D   1, 2 and 3

42 In an interlocking accounting system what would be the entry in the cost accounts to record the charging of indirect production labour costs?

	Debit	Credit
A	Cost ledger control	Production overhead
B	Production overhead	Wages
C	Wages	Financial ledger control
D	Work-in-progress	Wages

43 A company manufactures a single product. Unit costs are:

	$/Unit
Variable production	14·75
Fixed production	8·10
Variable selling	2·40
Fixed selling	5·35

400,000 units of the product were manufactured in a period, during which 394,000 units were sold. There was no inventory of the product at the beginning of the period.

Using marginal costing, what is the total value of the finished goods inventory at the end of the period?

A $88,500
B $102,900
C $137,100
D $183,600

44 Ordering lead times and weekly usage of a raw material are:

	Lead time	Weekly usage
Minimum	2 weeks	400 kg
Maximum	3 weeks	500 kg
Average	2½ weeks	450 kg

The economic order quantity of the material is 1,800 kg and the reorder level is 1,500 kg.

What is the minimum inventory control level?

A 300 kg
B 375 kg
C 675 kg
D 700 kg

45 Which of the following is NOT a feature of certificates of deposit?

A Fixed term
B Issued by a bank
C Non-negotiable
D Specified interest rate

46 Which of the following describes the margin of safety?

A The total sales units up to break-even sales volume
B The difference in units between the expected sales volume and the break-even sales volume
C The difference between sales value and variable costs
D The difference between total costs and the fixed costs at break-even sales volume

47 Which of the following statements explain how a cash budget can be used as a mechanism for control?

(1) Actual cash flows can be compared with budgeted cash flows to reveal variations from what was expected
(2) Cash budgets can be revised on a regular basis for forecasting purposes

A 1 only
B 2 only
C Both 1 and 2
D Neither 1 nor 2

48 In the manufacture of Chemical X there is a normal loss of 10% of the material input into the process. 340 litres of Chemical X were manufactured in a period during which there was an abnormal loss of 5% of the material input into the process.

How many litres of material were input into the process during the period?

A $378
B $289
C $306
D $400

49 The following information has been extracted from the records of a firm:

	Production department		
	Budget	Result	Variance
Direct materials	$1,231	$1,648	$427 Adv
Direct labour	$2,156	$1,972	$184 Fav
Direct expenses	$125	$142	$17 Adv

Consider the following statements:

(1) Overtime premium of direct labour caused direct expenses to increase
(2) Lower skilled direct labour was used causing increased usage of direct materials
(3) Higher quality of direct labour and materials were used enabling fewer direct labour hours to be required
(4) Higher skilled direct labour was used enabling less direct material to be used

Which of the statements are consistent with the variances shown?

A 2 and 3 only
B 3 and 4 only
C 1, 2 and 4 only
D 1, 2, 3 and 4

50 Which TWO of the following are usually treasury functions?

(1) Credit control
(2) Currency management
(3) Debt collection
(4) Investment of surplus funds

A 1 and 3
B 1 and 4
C 2 and 3
D 2 and 4

(100 marks)

End of Question Paper

Answers

1 B
2 C
3 C
4 A
5 C
   $57,200 – (5,200 x $50,000 ÷ 5,000 units) = $5,200 favourable
6 A
   (250/2)*3 = $375
7 C
8 B
   (166,200 – 5000)*20% = $32,240
9 D
   Expected output: (12,000*90%) = 10,800 units
   Total costs: (86,090 + 39,320) = $125,410
   Cost per kg of expected output: (125,410/10,800) = $11·61
10 D
11 C
   Relevant costs: (150 kg at opportunity cost of sale of $40) + (250 at $53) = $19,250
12 C
   Product C absorbed overheads: (120,000/12,500) = 9·6
13 B
14 C
   34,295 /((4*40*10) + (5*60*12) + (6 x 65 x 8)) = $4·12
15 A
16 A
17 C
18 B
   Indirect costs in year 2: (35,000 + 45,000) x 1·20 = $96,000
   Total area in year 2: (15,000 x 1·33) = 20,000
   Proportion of B: (5,000/20,000) = 0·25
   Cost apportioned to B: (96,000*0·25) = $24,000
19 D
20 C
   (1,500,000/120,000) = $12·50
21 B
22 A
   Contribution per unit: 70 – (29·50 + 4·80) = $35·7
   Total contribution: (19,700 * 35·7) = $703,290
23 A
   Overhead absorption rate: (20,000/4,000) = $5
   Absorbed overheads: (5*4,200) =$21,000
   Under absorbed: (21,000 – 21,840) = $840
24 A
25 C
26 D
   Using high low method: (51,652 – 47,328)/(2,900 – 2,400) = $8·65
27 B
28 D
29 A
   (724,000 + 206,900 – 4,360 – 241,600) = $684,940
30 A
   Direct materials: (5 kg*30,000) = 150,000 kg, available only 140,000 kg
   Direct labour: (11 hrs*30,000) = 330,000 hrs, available 340,000 hrs

31 A

Activity ratio = Efficiency ratio x Capacity ratio

(103·5/90)*100

32 D

33 C

34 C

(50 units at $6) + (20 units at $5·50) = $410

35 A

$20,000 – ($4,000 x 5·65) = $2,600

36 B

Number of units per day equivalent to guaranteed minimum daily wage: 45/0·6= 75

Received Mon, Wed and Friday: (90 + 75 + 90)*0·6) = $153

Tuesday and Thursday received a minimum of $45 = $90

Total earnings: (153 + 90) = $243

37 A

$15,972/1·1^3 = $12,000

38 D

	A	B	C	D
Contribution per skilled labour:	2 (2·8/1·4)	2·17	2·11	2·4
Ranking	4	2	3	1

39 D

40 D

41 A

42 B

43 A

(400,000 kg – 394,000 kg)*$14·75 = $88,500

44 B

Reorder level – (average lead-time * average usage)

1,500 – (2·5*450) = 375kg

45 C

46 B

47 A

48 D

Good output: (100% – 10% – 5%) = 85%

Input into the process: 340/·85 = 400 kg

49 A

50 D